KT-210-306

# ROSE JOTTER

**Dr. D.G. Hessayon**

1st Edition 200,000

**Other Books in the JOTTER Series:**
HOUSE PLANT JOTTER · VEGETABLE JOTTER

| Year: | Location: |
|-------|-----------|
|       |           |

pbi PUBLICATIONS · BRITANNICA HOUSE · WALTHAM CROSS · HERTS · ENGLAND

Printed and bound by Hazell Watson and Viney Limited Aylesbury Bucks. England

**ISBN 0 903505 27 4**

© D G HESSAYON 1989

# CHAPTER 1

# INTRODUCTION

## How to use this book

On each page you will find scores of facts to help you with your plants. Check up each time you decide to buy or have a new job to do. On many of the pages there are sections which are printed in blue — these are for you to fill in with your own information. In this way you can build up a permanent record and a useful reminder for next season.

No other flower quite captivates the heart in the same way as the rose. In the British garden it is the symbol of the flowering season — the first blooms tell you that summer has at last arrived.

Part of the fascination is that you can never remain an expert — you have to keep up to date. Each year new varieties appear and old favourites slip away — 60 per cent of the present top 10 Floribundas are children of the 1970s and 1980s. There is always something new to learn.

This book tells you the basic features of today's top 360 roses, based on their popularity with the rose growers. It is also chock-full of ideas on what to do and when to do it. And then there is the unique feature — the blue boxes for you to fill in.

## ROSE TYPES

### HYBRID TEA ROSES
The most popular rose type. Flowers are double, usually large and high-centred and borne singly or as a small group on the flower stem. Repeat flowering, with flushes from midsummer to late autumn.

For further details and varieties see pages 6–21.

### FLORIBUNDA ROSES
The second most popular rose type. Flower form varies widely — the key feature is the grouping of blooms into substantial trusses or clusters. Repeat flowering, with flowers from midsummer to late autumn.

For further details and varieties see pages 22–33.

### MINIATURES
A group of small bushes which grow 6–18 in. high. The mature height depends on the variety and propagation method — rooted cuttings are shorter than budded or grafted plants. To be a true Miniature the size of the leaves, flowers and stems should all be in proportion.

For further details and varieties see pages 34–35.

### CLIMBERS & RAMBLERS
The stems of this type are longer than those of bush roses and need some form of support. The Ramblers have lax stems, large trusses and just one flowering season. The Climbers have stiffer stems, smaller trusses and are often repeat flowering.

For further details and varieties see pages 36–41.

### SHRUB ROSES
Shrub Roses are the poor relations in the family of roses. They are so often regarded as too large and too old-fashioned for the modern garden. This is not so — it is true that few are suitable for bedding, but they do make excellent subjects for the shrub border. They are available in all shapes and sizes with blooms which can rival Hybrid Teas in shape and a small selection can provide blooms from May until late autumn. There are 3 basic groups:

●

SPECIES ROSES are wild roses and their close relatives. Many are known by their Latin names (e.g *Rosa rubrifolia*) but some have Common names (e.g *Canary Bird*). Most Species Roses bloom only once a year, but this flowering period may be as early as May.

OLD-FASHIONED ROSES generally date back to the time before Hybrid Teas or Floribundas, although both the Hybrid Musks and Rugosa Shrubs are 20th century creations. There are a number of families here and nearly all are represented in the catalogues. The **Rugosa Shrubs** are both important and useful — hardy, grow-anywhere toughness, wrinkled leaves, repeat flowering and remarkably disease-free. The **Albas** are also very useful as they withstand partial shade better than other roses. Sweetly scented with grey-green leaves, they produce a single midsummer flush. The **Bourbon Roses** have large and globular blooms which are filled with petals — the **China Roses** sold today are delicate and small-flowered plants. The **Moss Roses** bear sticky hairs and both the **Damask Roses** and **Hybrid Musks** are grown for their fragrance.

●

MODERN SHRUB ROSES are a widely diverse family with little in common apart from their 20th century origin. They range from dwarfs to giants and most, but not all, are repeat flowering. The shape of the blooms is usually modern rather than old-fashioned.

For further details and varieties see pages 42–49.

### PATIO ROSES
During the 1980s a new unofficial grouping appeared in the catalogues and magazines — the Patio Roses. These are dwarf bushes which grow about 18 in. high. They have a neat growth habit and in a true Patio Rose the leaves, flowers and stems should all be to scale.

The list is drawn from the low-growing Floribundas. Varieties which belong here are *Anna Ford, Bianco, Boys' Brigade, Gentle Touch, Marlena, Peek a Boo, Piccolo, Regensberg, Sweet Dream, Sweet Magic, Tip Top* and *Topsi*. Some growers include low-growing Shrub Roses such as *Nozomi* and *The Fairy*.

### GROUND COVER ROSES
The use of roses as ground cover plants has only recently gained popular appeal. Nowadays you will find a ground cover section in most catalogues — varieties which spread and form a dense leafy mat. These plants are weed suppressors, but never regard them as weed eliminators.

Ten ground cover roses are listed in the Shrub Roses section (pages 42–49). Some are spreading bushes with arching stems which cover the soil — examples are *Bonica, Fiona* and *Rosy Cushion*. Others are prostrate plants with stems which creep across the ground, such as *Nozomi, Max Graf* or *Swany*. If there is a large stretch of land to cover, use a 'game bird' variety such as *Grouse*.

### GRANDIFLORA ROSES
In the U.S. large Floribundas with shapely H.T blooms are called Grandifloras — *Queen Elizabeth* is the most notable example. This term has not gained popular appeal in Britain, although it has been adopted in a few catalogues to describe any tall-growing rose type in which the cluster habit and freedom of flowering of the Floribunda is combined with the classic flower form of the Hybrid Tea.

Such varieties are excellent for planting as a back-of-the-border bush, specimen plant or hedge. Included here are *Alexander, Chinatown, L'Oréal Trophy, Pink Parfait, Queen Elizabeth, Sea Pearl, Super Star* and *Uncle Walter*.

## FLOWERING PERIODS

### ONCE FLOWERING
A single flush of blooms is produced which generally lasts for several weeks. The usual time is June or July. Occasionally a few flowers appear in autumn, but this flowering is too sporadic to be regarded as a second flush.

### REPEAT FLOWERING
Two or more flushes of blooms are produced during the growing season. Repeat (also known as recurrent or remontant) varieties may produce some flowers between the main flushes — such roses are sometimes described as 'continuous' flowering.

## GROWTH TYPES

The four basic growth types are
**ground cover**, **bush**, **standard** and **climbing**.
A bush may be a Hybrid Tea, Floribunda or Shrub Rose

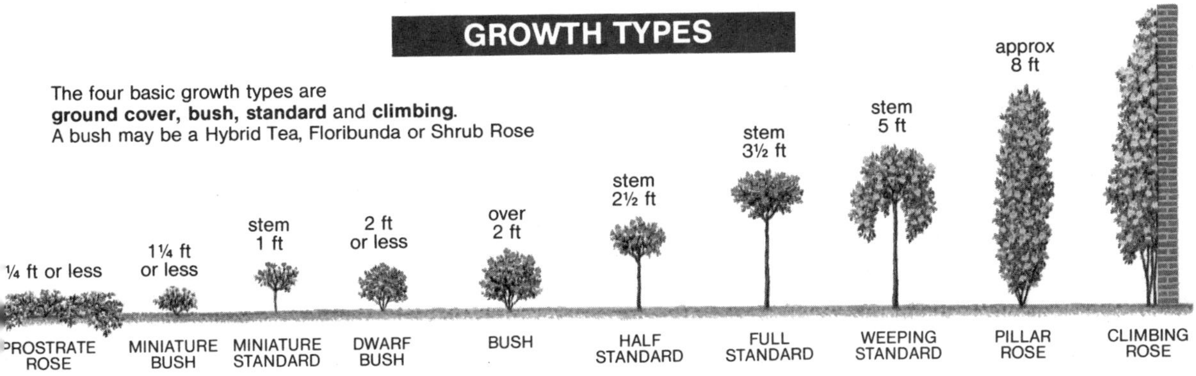

approx
8 ft

stem
5 ft

stem
3½ ft

stem
2½ ft

over
2 ft

2 ft
or less

stem
1 ft

1¼ ft
or less

¼ ft or less

PROSTRATE
ROSE | MINIATURE
BUSH | MINIATURE
STANDARD | DWARF
BUSH | BUSH | HALF
STANDARD | FULL
STANDARD | WEEPING
STANDARD | PILLAR
ROSE | CLIMBING
ROSE

## PLANT HEIGHTS

| Height of plant | HYBRID TEAS & FLORIBUNDAS | MINIATURES | CLIMBERS & RAMBLERS | SHRUB ROSES |
|---|---|---|---|---|
| **VERY SHORT** | under 1½ ft | ½ ft | | under 2 ft |
| **SHORT** | 1½ — 2½ ft | ¾ ft | under 10 ft | 2 — 3 ft |
| **SHORT-MEDIUM** | 2½ — 2¾ ft | | 10 — 12½ ft | 3 — 4½ ft |
| **MEDIUM** | 2¾ — 3½ ft | 1 ft | 12½ — 15 ft | 4½ — 5½ ft |
| **MEDIUM-TALL** | 3½ — 4 ft | 1¼ ft | 15 — 20 ft | 5½ — 7 ft |
| **TALL** | over 4 ft | 1½ ft | over 20 ft | over 7 ft |

## FLOWER TYPES

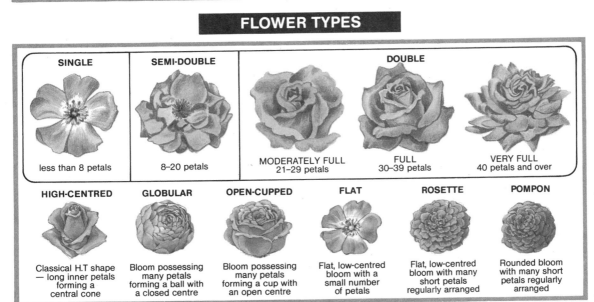

**SINGLE**
less than 8 petals

**SEMI-DOUBLE**
8–20 petals

**DOUBLE**

**MODERATELY FULL**
21–29 petals

**FULL**
30–39 petals

**VERY FULL**
40 petals and over

**HIGH-CENTRED**
Classical H.T shape — long inner petals forming a central cone

**GLOBULAR**
Bloom possessing many petals forming a ball with a closed centre

**OPEN-CUPPED**
Bloom possessing many petals forming a cup with an open centre

**FLAT**
Flat, low-centred bloom with a small number of petals

**ROSETTE**
Flat, low-centred bloom with many short petals regularly arranged

**POMPON**
Rounded bloom with many short petals regularly arranged

## FLOWER SIZES

| Diameter of flower | H.Ts, FLORIBUNDAS, CLIMBERS & SHRUBS | MINIATURES |
|---|---|---|
| **SMALL** | under 2½ in. | under 1 in. |
| **MEDIUM** | 2½ — 4½ in. | 1 — 1¾ in. |
| **LARGE** | over 4½ in. | over 1¾ in. |

# ROSE GARDEN PLANS

Draw the outline of your rose bed or border and use the plan either to record the bushes which are present or your ideas for the future. Mark up the references (e.g C–21, T–4) against the appropriate varieties listed in the A–Z sections beginning on page 6. When marking out your proposals for new plantings, check the recommended distances (page 52) between roses.

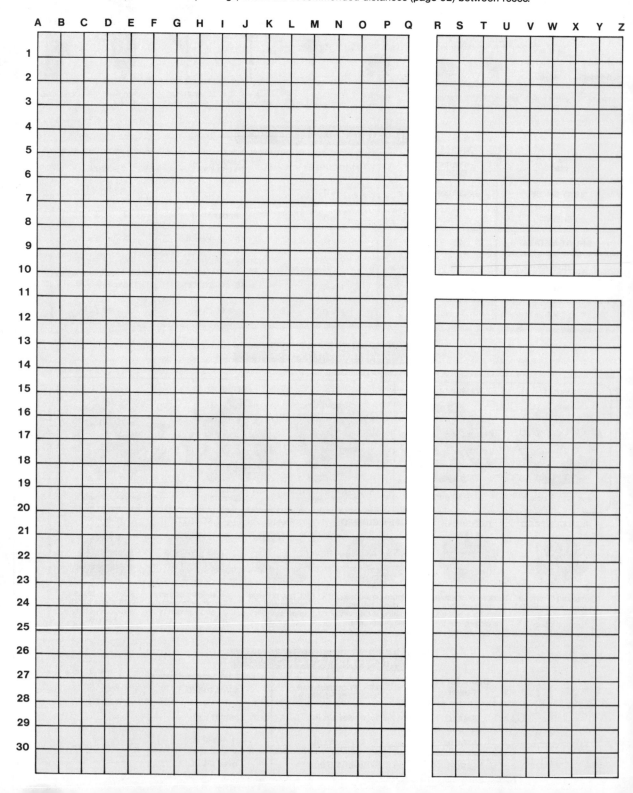

# CHAPTER 2
# VARIETIES

**INCLUDED IN ROSE ANALYSIS**
The Royal National Rose Society carries out a survey each year to find out, in the opinion of its members, the best roses available in the various classes and for various uses. Inclusion in the Analysis therefore means that at least some of the keener rose growers in Britain consider the variety worthy of mention.

**BLF** Included in the top 26 Best Large-Flowered (H.T) Roses

**DR** Included in the top 10 for Disease Resistance

**N** Included in the top 13 New Roses

**SH** Included in the top 25 Shrub Roses and others used as Shrubs

**BCF** Included in the top 24 Best Cluster-Flowered (Floribunda) Roses

**OGR** Included in the top 11 Old Garden Roses

**SC** Included in the top 13 Scented Roses

**C & R** Included in the top 23 Climbers and Ramblers

**E** Included in the top 23 Exhibition Roses

**No** Not included

**VARIETIES** About 2000 different varieties are currently available — about 360 are listed in this Jotter. These are not the "best" roses — they have been chosen on the basis of their popularity in catalogues, shops and stores. Both good and bad features are described

**AVAILABILITY** There are 73 members of the Rose Growers Association. Availability is listed on the basis of the percentage of members offering the variety:

| | |
|---|---|
| under 5% | ★ |
| 5–25% | ★★ |
| 25–50% | ★★★ |
| 50–75% | ★★★★ |
| over 75% | ★★★★★ |

**HEIGHT** See table on page 3

**RESISTANCE TO DISEASE** Resistance to mildew and/or black spot is listed as good, average or poor. "Poor" varieties require regular spraying

**SIZE OF BLOOMS** See table on page 3

Included in Rose Analysis

E

**GARDEN RECORD**

Performance during the year

Problems during the year

A bit of rain damage in July

Grown in garden

Year of planting (if known)

Supplier

Good

Cocker

?

Flowers didn't open in rain — will have to go!!!

Poor — few flowers

Byways G.C.

1984

Mauve

**HYBRID TEA ROSES**

**PLANT DETAILS**

**BLOOM DETAILS**

| Year of introduction | Height | Resistance to disease | Availability | Size of blooms Number of petals | Colour Fragrance |
|---|---|---|---|---|---|
| | | | | Large 70 petals | Scarlet: pale scarlet reverse Fragrant |
| 1967 | Medium | Good | ★★★★ | Medium 30 petals | Deep red Fragrant |
| 1987 | Medium | Good | ★★★★ | Medium 30 petals | Ruby red Slightly fragrant |
| 1979 | Short | Average | ★★★ | Medium 35 petals | Orange vermilion Fragrant |
| 1960 | Medium-tall | Poor | ★★★★ | | |

Pink

Lilac

The search for the blue rose goes on — the listed 'blues' are really lilacs and mauves. Sometimes attractive, but more often these blooms look dull and faded when you will find very few in the catalogues.

BONSOIR

| | | | | Medium petals | Silvery lilac Very fragrant |
|---|---|---|---|---|---|
| 1964 | Medium | Average | ★★★★★ | Large | |

lacs

E MOON
best of the 'blue' roses
he fragrance is strong and

E PARFUM

Note down your views on performance. A poor showing in a single season may be due to the weather — poor performance over several years indicates that it is time to replace the variety

Note plant or bloom details of the unlisted variety if you know them

Mark your rose varieties with a red tick. Use a pencil to tick varieties which you propose to buy in the near future

Write in the name of the supplier — grower, garden centre, DIY store etc. This information is useful if you have cause to complain at a later date

Problems should be noted as they occur — they will help you next year. If black spot is a problem, put on the first spray as leaf buds open next year

Write in the name of any unlisted variety which you are growing or propose to grow in the garden. The fact that a rose is not listed means that it is not offered by many growers — this can be due to recent introduction, lack of public appeal, poor growth properties or just lack of general recognition for a perfectly good rose

# HYBRID TEA ROSES

## Varieties

| | PLANT DETAILS | | | | BLOOM DETAILS | |
|---|---|---|---|---|---|---|
| | Year of introduction | Height | Resistance to disease | Availability | Size of blooms — Number of petals | Colour Fragran |

### Whites & Creams

Very few varieties are pure white — *Message* is perhaps the best example. Some H.Ts occasio have a pinkish or buff tinge (*Virgo, Pascali* etc) — others always do (e.g *Elizabeth Harkness, Pri* A few varieties (e.g *Evening Star, Peaudouce*) have petals with a pale yellow base.

| | | | | | | |
|---|---|---|---|---|---|---|
| **ELIZABETH HARKNESS**<br>Large, sweet-smelling flowers appear early in the season — regarded as one of the best of all creamy H.Ts. Good for cutting | 1969 | Short-medium | Average | ★★ | Large — 35 petals | Ivory, shaded p — Fragran |
| **EVENING STAR**<br>Much was expected from this white fragrant rose from the U.S., but it failed to live up to its early promise. It is no longer recommended | 1977 | Medium-tall | Average | ★★ | Large — 25 petals | White; yel at base — Fragran |
| **MESSAGE**<br>It has its good points — pure white, high-centred blooms etc, but not recommended. Leaves are very susceptible to mildew and blooms are spoilt by rain | 1956 | Short | Poor | ★★ | Medium — 35 petals | White — Slightly fragran |
| **PASCALI**<br>Still a wise choice. Good rain resistance for a white rose and blooms are long lasting. Excellent for cutting, but bushes look spindly | 1963 | Medium-tall | Average | ★★★★★ | Medium — 25 petals | White — Slightly fragran |
| **PEAUDOUCE**<br>A new star of the white rose world — it's a popular choice. Attractive leafy bushes bear large and fragrant porcelain-like flowers | 1985 | Medium | Good | ★★★ | Large — 40 petals | Ivory; yell at base — Fragran |
| **POLAR STAR**<br>Another modern white — Rose of the Year in 1985. Outstanding for showing, cutting and general display — unfortunately there is no scent | 1982 | Medium-tall | Good | ★★★★★ | Medium — 35 petals | White — No fragra |
| **PRISTINE**<br>Health is good, blooms are large with a strong scent and there are no obvious drawbacks. Even so, it's not a best-seller | 1978 | Medium-tall | Good | ★★ | Large — 25 petals | Ivory, shaded p — Very fragr |
| **SILVER WEDDING**<br>A compact bedding and cutting rose which bears its blooms in clusters rather than singly. Not pure white — there is a pinkish or orange blush | 1976 | Short-medium | Good | ★★★ | Medium — 35 petals | Creamy w — Slightly fragran |
| **VIRGO**<br>For 30 years gardeners who wanted a white H.T picked *Virgo*. Now its time is over — today's *Virgo* has gaunt growth, few flowers and mildewed leaves | 1947 | Short | Poor | ★★ | Medium — 30 petals | White — Slightly fragran |

### Yellows

There are some pure yellows — examples are *King's Ransom* and *Miss Harp*. Some are golden rath than yellow and the dividing line between 'yellows' and 'oranges' is a blurred one. So is the dividing line between the pink-shaded yellows (e.g *Sutter's Gold*) and the blends (e.g *The Lady*).

| | | | | | | |
|---|---|---|---|---|---|---|
| **BELLE BLONDE**<br>Once a favourite yellow bedding rose, but no longer popular. The flowers still hold their colour remarkably well, but disease and declining vigour are problems | 1955 | Short | Poor | ★★ | Medium — 35 petals | Golden yellow — Fragran |
| **BUCCANEER**<br>This tall variety (4–5 ft) has disappeared from almost all the catalogues, and is not really worth searching for. Flowers are borne in trusses | 1953 | Tall | Average | ★ | Medium — 30 petals | Buttercu yellow — Slightly frag |
| **CITY OF GLOUCESTER**<br>Recommended as an outstanding exhibition variety in the 1970s — now it is not recommended by anybody. Too tall and too dull for the average garden | 1969 | Tall | Average | ★ | Large — 35 petals | Saffron yellow — No fragra |
| **DIORAMA**<br>If only the blooms did not blow so quickly. Even so, it is a highly recommended variety. Blooms early and abundantly — flowers stand up to rain | 1965 | Medium | Average | ★★ | Large — 30 petals | Deep yell shaded p — Fragran |
| **DR A J VERHAGE**<br>A small and upright rose, excellent for growing under glass but a poor choice for the garden. It can be killed by severe winter weather | 1960 | Short | Average | ★★ | Medium — 25 petals | Yellow, sha apricot — Fragrant |
| **DUTCH GOLD**<br>A good choice if you want large, strongly-scented blooms. The colour is golden rather than yellow and the colour does not fade with age | 1978 | Medium | Good | ★★★ | Large — 35 petals | Golden yellow — Very fragr |

A chance cross between a Tea Rose and a Hybrid Perpetual gave rise to the first Hybrid Tea *(La France)* in 1867. This group is now the most popular of all rose types, and is available in both bush and standard form. The flower stems are long and the blooms are shapely. The typical Hybrid Tea bears blooms which are medium-sized or large, with many petals forming a distinct central cone. The blooms are borne singly or with several side shoots. The World Federation of Rose Societies prefers the name 'Large-flowered Roses' for this group, but the ordinary gardener does not.

VARIETIES

## GARDEN RECORD

| Grown in garden | Year of planting (if known) | Supplier | Performance during the year | Problems during the year | Included in Rose Analysis |
|---|---|---|---|---|---|
| White | | Creamy white | | Ivory | |
| | | | | | No |
| | | | | | No |
| | | | | | No |
| | | | | | BLF |
| | | | | | N |
| | | | | | N |
| | | | | | No |
| | | | | | No |
| | | | | | No |
| | | | | | |
| Primrose yellow | | Canary yellow | | Golden yellow | Buttercup yellow |
| | | | | | No |
| | | | | | No |
| | | | | | No |
| | | | | | No |
| | | | | | No |
| | | | | | No |

# HYBRID TEA ROSES

## Varieties
### Yellows continued

| | PLANT DETAILS | | | | BLOOM DETAILS | |
|---|---|---|---|---|---|---|
| | Year of introduction | Height | Resistance to disease | Availability | Size of blooms — Number of petals | Colour Fragrance |
| **FRAGRANT GOLD**<br>Good scent and a bright colour, but it has not become a best-seller. The problem is a shortage of petals — the public likes full blooms | 1982 | Medium | Average | ★★ | Medium — 15 petals | Deep yellow — Very fragrant |
| **FRED GIBSON**<br>*Fred Gibson* has won many prizes on the show bench, but it is now in few catalogues. A notable exhibition variety, but far too spindly for bedding | 1966 | Medium | Average | ★ | Large — 30 petals | Amber yellow — Slightly fragrant |
| **FREEDOM**<br>This one is expected to become one of the stars of the 1990s. It has outstanding bedding as well as show-bench qualities. Compact and bushy | 1984 | Short-medium | Good | ★★★ | Medium — 30 petals | Deep yellow — Fragrant |
| **GOLD CROWN**<br>Blooms are very large and the stems are long and straight. A big and strong variety with one drawback — it often starts to bloom later than most H.Ts | 1960 | Tall | Average | ★★ | Large — 35 petals | Deep yellow — Slightly fragrant |
| **GOLDEN DAYS**<br>Classic-shaped golden flowers appear freely on the leafy bushes. No problems, but petals are not plentiful and there are not many suppliers | 1981 | Medium | Good | ★★ | Medium — 25 petals | Deep yellow — Slightly fragrant |
| **GOLDEN TIMES**<br>This rose of the 1970s fell out of the catalogues during the 1980s. It has no serious garden faults but it is taller than average and there are no special points | 1972 | Medium-tall | Average | ★★ | Large — 50 petals | Yellow — Fragrant |
| **GOLDSTAR**<br>An H.T of the 1980s which appeals to flower arrangers — the stems are long and straight. Growth is upright rather than bushy and flowers appear freely | 1982 | Medium | Good | ★★ | Medium — 30 petals | Deep yellow — Slightly fragrant |
| **GRANDPA DICKSON**<br>After more than 20 years it is still regarded as one of the best pale yellow H.Ts for cutting and exhibiting. Sometimes looks rather spindly | 1966 | Medium | Good | ★★★★★ | Large — 35 petals | Lemon yellow — Slightly fragrant |
| **KING'S RANSOM**<br>Another variety of the 1960s which has kept its virtues. It remains one of the best pure yellows you can buy. An excellent bedding rose which flowers freely | 1961 | Medium | Good | ★★★★★ | Large — 40 petals | Yellow — Fragrant |
| **LOLITA**<br>Long stems make it a good rose for cutting —blooms last well in water. It never became a popular rose and now has nearly disappeared from the catalogues | 1972 | Medium-tall | Average | ★ | Medium — 30 petals | Deep gold — Fragrant |
| **MIDAS**<br>A LeGrice rose which won awards in Britain and Holland but has remained a rarity. Growth is upright rather than bushy and the flowers appear freely | 1980 | Medium-tall | Good | ★ | Large — 45 petals | Yellow — Slightly fragrant |
| **MISS HARP**<br>Some experts thought that this variety would challenge *King's Ransom* for the pure yellow crown. It never did, but it is a reliable variety which appeals to flower arrangers | 1970 | Medium | Average | ★★ | Medium — 40 petals | Deep yellow — Fragrant |
| **POT O' GOLD**<br>A bushy plant which flowers freely. Good for bedding and cutting — some growers believe that it will be the outstanding fragrant yellow of the future | 1982 | Medium | Good | ★★★ | Medium — 30 petals | Old gold — Very fragrant |
| **SIMBA**<br>The blooms are outstanding — large and high-centred. The plant is also attractive — compact and leafy. The only drawback is the distinct gap between flushes | 1981 | Short-medium | Good | ★★★ | Large — 30 petals | Yellow — Slightly fragrant |
| **SUMMER SUNSHINE**<br>The catalogue photograph makes it look a winner — brilliant yellow, large and long-stemmed. Think before buying. It is unreliable and often short-lived | 1962 | Medium | Average | ★★ | Medium — 35 petals | Deep yellow — Slightly fragrant |
| **SUNBLEST**<br>Highly recommended for bedding and cutting. The flowers are bright and unfading but the scent is slight. Upright rather than bushy — vigorous and reliable | 1970 | Medium | Good | ★★★ | Medium — 30 petals | Yellow — Slightly fragrant |
| **SUTTER'S GOLD**<br>This sweet-scented variety has kept its place in some catalogues for 40 years. An old favourite, but stems are lanky, leaves are few and flowers soon fade | 1950 | Medium | Average | ★★ | Large — 30 petals | Yellow, shaded pink — Very fragrant |
| **YELLOW PAGES**<br>Hardly anyone sells it these days, despite its early promise. Easy to grow with large blooms on compact bushes. The problem — flowers have confused centres | 1972 | Short-medium | Good | ★ | Large — 45 petals | Yellow, shaded pink — Slightly fragrant |
| | | | | | | |
| | | | | | | |
| | | | | | | |

| Grown in garden | Year of planting (if known) | Supplier | Performance during the year | Problems during the year | Included in Rose Analysis |
|---|---|---|---|---|---|
| | | | | | No |
| | | | | | E |
| | | | | | No |
| | | | | | No |
| | | | | | No |
| | | | | | No |
| | | | | | No |
| | | | | | BLF DR E |
| | | | | | BLF |
| | | | | | No |
| | | | | | No |
| | | | | | No |
| | | | | | No |
| | | | | | No |
| | | | | | No |
| | | | | | No |
| | | | | | BLF SC |
| | | | | | No |
| | | | | | |
| | | | | | |
| | | | | | |

**GARDEN RECORD**

VARIETIES

# HYBRID TEA ROSES

## Varieties

| | PLANT DETAILS | | | | BLOOM DETAILS | |
|---|---|---|---|---|---|---|
| | Year of introduction | Height | Resistance to disease | Availability | Size of blooms — Number of petals | Colou... Fragranc... |

### Oranges & Blends

'Orange' is not a precise description and the boundaries are ill-defined. Some experts would include *Beauté* with the yellows and others might move *Cheshire Life* to the reds. 'Blends' is an even vaguer term — it means that there are at least 2 distinct colours on each

| Variety | Year of introduction | Height | Resistance to disease | Availability | Size of blooms — Number of petals | Colour Fragrance |
|---|---|---|---|---|---|---|
| **ADOLF HORSTMANN** Colourful, large and fragrant but it is found in few catalogues. It is upright rather than bushy and often fails to bloom freely. No longer a good choice | 1971 | Medium-tall | Good | ★★ | Large — 25 petals | Bronze, ed... pink Fragran... |
| **ALPINE SUNSET** A sturdy and reliable variety with scented globular flowers. A good choice if you want a peachy rose for general garden display. Flowers are freely produced | 1972 | Medium | Good | ★★★ | Large — 30 petals | Peach, blen... yellow Very fragra... |
| **APRICOT SILK** Low disease resistance takes this one out of the good buy list. It's a pity — the petals are silky and the buds are elegant | 1965 | Medium-tall | Poor | ★★★ | Large — 20 petals | Apricot, ble... orange Slightly frag... |
| **BASILDON BOND** Not many growers offer *Basildon Bond*, but it is worth looking for. It blooms earlier than other H.Ts, and the buds are richly veined in red | 1980 | Medium | Average | ★★ | Large — 25 petals | Apricot Fragran... |
| **BEAUTE** A low bedding rose with a rather delicate constitution. Its glory is the display of beautiful buds. Good for flower arranging, but these buds open into loose flowers | 1954 | Short | Poor | ★★ | Medium — 25 petals | Golden ap... Slightly fragran... |
| **BETTINA** An excellent rose for cutting and flower arranging, but avoid it if your garden is prone to black spot. Vigorous, free-flowering and resistant to rain | 1953 | Short-medium | Poor | ★★★ | Medium — 35 petals | Orange, ve... bronze Fragran... |
| **CAN CAN** A good variety for the front of the border. The flowers are nothing special, but they appear early in the season and are borne in large numbers | 1982 | Short | Average | ★★★ | Large — 20 petals | Orange sc... Fragran... |
| **CHAMPION** The typical show-bench rose — large, fragrant, classic-shaped and colourful. No longer a best-seller — it is prone to disease attack these days | 1976 | Short-medium | Poor | ★★ | Large — 50 petals | Gold, flush... pink and... Very fragr... |
| **CHESHIRE LIFE** Orange or red — it's a borderline colour. A good choice if you like pale vermilion — this one resists disease and stands up to cold and rain | 1972 | Short | Good | ★★★ | Large — 35 petals | Vermilio... orange... Slightly frag... |
| **CHICAGO PEACE** Here is one for bedding, hedging or exhibiting. You will need space — it grows 4–5 ft tall. A colourful sport of *Peace* with saucer-sized blooms | 1962 | Tall | Average | ★★★★ | Large — 45 petals | Pink, copp... and yello... Slightly frag... |
| **DORIS TYSTERMAN** An attractive orange-red variety which blooms freely and does especially well in autumn. Growth is upright and foliage is bronzy — disease is the only problem | 1975 | Medium | Poor | ★★★★★ | Medium — 30 petals | Tangerin... darker at e... Slightly frag... |
| **DOUBLE DELIGHT** "Like a vanilla ice dipped in strawberry juice" according to one of the catalogues. Free-flowering — outstanding for cutting. Mildew can be a problem | 1977 | Medium | Poor | ★★★★ | Large — 40 petals | Creamy w... edged re... Very fragra... |
| **HELEN TRAUBEL** No longer in the popular catalogues and no longer recommended. Beautiful buds and heavy fragrance, but these buds turn into open, drooping flowers | 1952 | Medium-tall | Average | ★★ | Large — 25 petals | Apricot, blended p... Very fragra... |
| **JOHNNIE WALKER** There are a number of large-flowered, sweetly-scented H.Ts — this is the one to buy if you are looking for hardiness. It shrugs off cold, disease and rain | 1982 | Medium-tall | Good | ★★ | Large — 20 petals | Apricot Very fragra... |
| **JULIA'S ROSE** A rose for the flower arranger — the elongated buds open slowly to produce porcelain-like flowers. Not for general garden display — the stems look gaunt | 1976 | Short | Average | ★★★ | Medium — 25 petals | Copper-tin... parchme... No fragra... |
| **JUST JOEY** You can't mistake this one — look for the frilly petals and pale edges. A best-seller for many years — vigorous and rain-resistant with a prolonged flowering season | 1973 | Short-medium | Good | ★★★★★ | Medium — 30 petals | Coppery or... paler at e... Fragran... |
| **LINCOLN CATHEDRAL** The 1985 Gold Medal of the RNRS went to this amateur-bred rose. Flowers are large, fragrant and colourful, borne in profusion above dark green foliage | 1987 | Medium | Good | ★★★ | Large — 30 petals | Deep pink; centre Fragran... |
| **L'OREAL TROPHY** A sport of *Alexander* with the same growth habits and healthy constitution. The flowers are a luminescent orange, but most growers have ignored it | 1982 | Tall | Good | ★★ | Large — 25 petals | Orange... Slightly fragran... |
| **LOVERS' MEETING** A new colour — clear Indian orange according to the catalogues. Vigorous and upright with bronze-tinted leaves — the blooms often occur in small trusses | 1980 | Medium | Good | ★★★★ | Medium — 30 petals | Tangerin... orange... Slightly frag... |
| **MICHELE MEILLAND** Far too delicate in appearance to win popular appeal. The buds are slim and the flowers rather small. It is hard to believe that it is an offspring of *Peace* | 1945 | Medium | Average | ★★ | Medium — 40 petals | Salmon, flu... pink Slightly frag... |

| Grown in garden | Year of planting (if known) | Supplier | Performance during the year | Problems during the year | Included in Rose Analysis |
|---|---|---|---|---|---|
| Apricot | | Salmon | Peach | Tangerine | Blend |
| | | | | | No |
| | | | | | No |
| | | | | | No |
| | | | | | No |
| | | | | | No |
| | | | | | No |
| | | | | | No |
| | | | | | E |
| | | | | | No |
| | | | | | No |
| | | | | | BLF |
| | | | | | BLF |
| | | | | | No |
| | | | | | No |
| | | | | | No |
| | | | | | BLF |
| | | | | | No |
| | | | | | No |
| | | | | | No |
| | | | | | No |

**GARDEN RECORD**

VARIETIES

# HYBRID TEA ROSES

## Varieties

### Oranges & Blends continued

| Variety | Year of introduction | Height | Resistance to disease | Availability | Size of blooms — Number of petals | Colour — Fragrance |
|---|---|---|---|---|---|---|
| **MISCHIEF** — The colour of this popular bedding variety is hard to describe. Early flowers are pale pink — late flowers have a distinctly orange colour. Profuse flowering is its special virtue | 1961 | Medium | Poor | ★★★★ | Medium — 30 petals | Coral salm — Slightly fragrant |
| **MOJAVE** — There are good points — flowers are plentiful and colourful, the bushes are hardy and the stems are long and thornless. But growth is leggy and flowers quickly blow | 1954 | Medium | Average | ★★ | Medium — 25 petals | Deep oran veined re — Slightly frag |
| **MRS SAM McGREDY** — In its time *Mrs Sam* was a great favourite, but it is now at the end of its commercial life. The vigour has gone and it is susceptible to disease | 1929 | Short-medium | Poor | ★ | Large — 40 petals | Coppery ora flushed re — Fragran |
| **PAUL SHIRVILLE** — Widely available and highly recommended. There is an unusual blend of colours — pink, salmon and peach. The blooms are high-centred and growth is vigorous | 1983 | Medium | Average | ★★★★ | Large — 30 petals | Salmon pi peach at b — Very fragra |
| **PEACE** — Surely the most famous of all roses. The blessings are still there — huge blooms, free-flowering etc. So are the drawbacks — flowering starts late and shoots are occasionally blind | 1942 | Tall | Good | ★★★★★ | Large — 45 petals | Yellow, edg pink — Slightly frag |
| **PEER GYNT** — A yellow rose at first, but the petals turn progressively pink with age. Flowering starts early and continues throughout the summer and autumn. Mildew is a problem | 1968 | Medium | Poor | ★★★ | Large — 40 petals | Canary yel flushed pi — Slightly frag |
| **PERFECTA** — An exhibitor's rose. Here are blooms to win prizes — large and high-centred. Not recommended for bedding — early flowers are unattractive and summer flowers droop | 1957 | Medium | Average | ★★ | Large — 65 petals | Cream, edge flushed crim — Slightly frag |
| **REBECCA CLAIRE** — Few varieties had a better start in life. It came to the market with both of the RNRS top awards and with unusual colouring, pronounced perfume and classic-shaped blooms | 1986 | Medium | Good | ★★★ | Large — 30 petals | Light copp blended cora — Very fragr |
| **REMEMBER ME** — This rose of the mid 1980s is widely grown and is expected to become increasingly popular. Each flower is held firmly on a stiff stalk in wide-spreading trusses | 1984 | Medium | Good | ★★★★ | Large — 25 petals | Coppery ora blended ye — Fragran |
| **ROSEMARY HARKNESS** — An excellent bedding rose — the shrubby plant is densely clothed with large leaves and the flowers open wide when mature. These blooms are borne singly or in clusters | 1985 | Medium | Good | ★★★ | Medium — 35 petals | Orange yel blended sal — Fragran |
| **ROYAL ROMANCE** — A lovely colour and classically-shaped blooms. The dark leaves make an ideal foil but it seems to lack popular appeal. Its time will come, say the growers | 1981 | Short-medium | Good | ★★ | Medium — 30 petals | Salmon pe — Fragrant |
| **SHOT SILK** — The unique colour is the reason why this old favourite keeps its place in some catalogues. The bush form is disappointing these days — choose *Climbing Shot Silk* instead | 1924 | Short | Average | ★★ | Medium — 30 petals | Salmon pi shaded go — Very fragra |
| **SILVER JUBILEE** — Quite rightly one of the stars of the H.T world. You will find all the virtues described in the catalogues — free-flowering, non-fading, luxurious foliage etc | 1978 | Short-medium | Good | ★★★★★ | Large — 25 petals | Coppery sal pink, shaded — Fragrant |
| **SOLITAIRE** — A statuesque rose, according to the catalogues. It is rather like a smaller version of *Peace*, to which it is not related. It is expected to become a popular bedding rose in the 1990s | 1986 | Medium-tall | Good | ★★ | Medium — 30 petals | Yellow, edg pink — Slightly frag |
| **SWEET PROMISE** — This is the flesh-coloured rose (*Sonia*) of the florist shop. Best grown under glass — it is distinctly unhappy outdoors in cold and wet districts | 1973 | Medium | Average | ★★ | Small — 30 petals | Rosy salm — Slightly fragrant |
| **THE LADY** — A new one for the exhibitor — the flowers are large and beautifully shaped. Petals are reflexed and the colour is unusual. Flowers are borne freely over a long period | 1986 | Tall | Good | ★★ | Large — 35 petals | Honey yell edged salm — Slightly frag |
| **TROIKA** — An excellent bedding variety. The best of the copper-coloured roses — flowering starts early in the season and the colour does not fade with age | 1972 | Medium | Good | ★★★ | Large — 30 petals | Orange bro shaded re — Fragran |
| **TYPHOON** — An eye-catching blend of pinks, copper and yellow. A good bedding rose, especially in autumn. Large, globular blooms appear on the compact bushes | 1972 | Short-medium | Good | ★★ | Large — 35 petals | Pink and co yellow at b — Fragran |
| **WHISKY MAC** — A top seller, proving that bright colour and strong scent can overcome drawbacks like disease susceptibility, unreliability in some soils and blooms which are open-cupped | 1967 | Medium | Poor | ★★★★★ | Medium — 30 petals | Golden apr — Very fragra |

| GARDEN RECORD | | | | | Included in Rose Analysis |
|---|---|---|---|---|---|
| Grown in garden | Year of planting (if known) | Supplier | Performance during the year | Problems during the year | |
| | | | | | BLF |
| | | | | | No |
| | | | | | No |
| | | | | | N |
| | | | | | BLF DR E |
| | | | | | No |
| | | | | | No |
| | | | | | No |
| | | | | | N |
| | | | | | N |
| | | | | | No |
| | | | | | No |
| | | | | | BLF DR E |
| | | | | | No |
| | | | | | No |
| | | | | | No |
| | | | | | BLF E |
| | | | | | No |
| | | | | | BLF SC |
| | | | | | |
| | | | | | |

VARIETIES

# HYBRID TEA ROSES

## Varieties

| | PLANT DETAILS | | | | BLOOM DETAILS | |
|---|---|---|---|---|---|---|
| | Year of introduction | Height | Resistance to disease | Availability | Size of blooms Number of petals | Colour Fragrance |

### Pinks

Pinks come in many shades, ranging from the near whites such as *Ophelia* to the near reds like *Mullard Jubilee*. Some are true pinks — examples include *Dr MacAlpine* and *Madame Butterfl* Others like *Blessings* are borderline oranges or blends.

| | Year of introduction | Height | Resistance to disease | Availability | Size of blooms Number of petals | Colour Fragrance |
|---|---|---|---|---|---|---|
| **ADMIRAL RODNEY** <br> This one is for the exhibitor. The flowers are large and the shape is good. Not for garden display — it isn't a free-flowering variety | 1973 | Medium | Good | ★★ | Large 45 petals | Rose pin Very fragra |
| **BLESSINGS** <br> It is the number of flowers which makes this an outstanding variety. The blooms are borne in clusters from early in the season until late autumn | 1968 | Medium | Good | ★★★★★ | Medium 30 petals | Coral pin Fragran |
| **CONGRATULATIONS** <br> Good for hedging and for cutting — long buds are borne on stout stems. It has never been a really popular variety — the colour fades with age | 1978 | Medium-tall | Good | ★★★ | Medium 40 petals | Rose pin Slightly fragrant |
| **DR MACALPINE** <br> Choose this one for the front of the border — it grows about 2 ft tall. The flowers are borne in trusses, so plenty of colour and fragrance are provided | 1983 | Short | Average | ★★ | Large 30 petals | Deep pin Very fragra |
| **HEIDI JAYNE** <br> One of the newer pinks — an upright bush with glossy leaves. The colour is bright and the flower shape is excellent. A candidate for 1990s popularity | 1987 | Medium | Good | ★★ | Large 35 petals | Deep pin Very fragra |
| **LADY SYLVIA** <br> No longer recommended for bedding — leaves are rather sparse. It still has its friends amongst flower arrangers — the long-stemmed flowers are attractive and sweetly scented | 1927 | Medium | Average | ★★ | Medium 30 petals | Pale pink yellow at b Very fragra |
| **LOVELY LADY** <br> Large, fragrant and fully double. A recent addition to the pink H.T range — good for bedding and perhaps for showing. Leaves are large and numerous | 1986 | Medium | Good | ★★ | Large 35 petals | Rose pin Fragran |
| **MADAME BUTTERFLY** <br> A much-loved old variety. The flowers make up in quantity for what they lack in size. Not a good buy — much of the beauty has been lost | 1918 | Short-medium | Average | ★★ | Medium 30 petals | Pale pink yellow at b Very fragra |
| **MARY DONALDSON** <br> The flowers are not very large and growth tends to be upright rather than bushy. A good cutting rose — the fragrant blooms are beautifully shaped | 1984 | Medium | Average | ★★ | Medium 40 petals | Salmon pi Fragran |
| **MULLARD JUBILEE** <br> A fine bedding rose — the blooms are exceptionally large and full of petals. The scent is quite strong and it does well under poor conditions | 1970 | Medium | Average | ★★ | Large 40 petals | Deep rose Fragran |
| **OPHELIA** <br> An old beauty with petals of palest pink. There is the heady scent of old roses. Not a strong plant — avoid it if your garden is exposed | 1912 | Short-medium | Average | ★★ | Medium 30 petals | Pale pink yellow at b Very fragra |
| **PINK FAVOURITE** <br> A good choice for bedding and showing. The blooms are large and high-centred, and the bushes have high resistance to mildew. Flowering starts later than the average H.T | 1956 | Medium | Good | ★★★★ | Large 30 petals | Deep pin Slightly fragrant |
| **PINK PEACE** <br> Bold blooms crammed with petals — just what you would expect from a child of *Peace*. Unlike *Peace* it has fragrance, upright growth and bronzy foliage | 1959 | Medium-tall | Good | ★★★ | Large 55 petals | Deep pin Fragran |
| **PRIMA BALLERINA** <br> Catalogues tell you the good points — lovely buds, attractive sweet-smelling flowers and stately growth. Remember, however, it is prone to mildew and is not free-flowering | 1958 | Medium-tall | Poor | ★★★★★ | Medium 25 petals | Cherry pin Very fragra |
| **ROYAL HIGHNESS** <br> Pearly-pink blooms with a porcelain-like look. Excellent if you are after prizes, but not for general garden display. It suffers badly in wet weather | 1962 | Medium | Poor | ★★★ | Large 40 petals | Flesh pin Fragran |
| **SILVER LINING** <br> The blooms last well in water, so it is sometimes recommended for cutting. Not a good choice — it is disease-prone and no longer flowers freely | 1958 | Medium | Poor | ★★ | Large 30 petals | Silvery pin Very fragra |
| **SUSAN HAMPSHIRE** <br> Unlike *Wendy Cussons*, this bright pink rose has not caught the public fancy. Surprising perhaps — health, flower size, fragrance and vigour are all good | 1974 | Medium | Good | ★★ | Large 40 petals | Fuchsia pin Fragran |
| **WENDY CUSSONS** <br> Highly praised and very popular. The colour is bright — too bright for some. Perfume and flower form are outstanding, and so are freedom of flowering and rain-resistance | 1959 | Medium | Good | ★★★★★ | Large 35 petals | Deep redd pink Very fragra |

| GARDEN RECORD | | | | | Included in Rose Analysis |
|---|---|---|---|---|---|
| Grown in garden | Year of planting (if known) | Supplier | Performance during the year | Problems during the year | |
| 🌹 Pink | | 🌹 Shell pink | | 🌹 Rose pink | 🌹 Carmine pink |
| | | | | | E |
| | | | | | BLF |
| | | | | | No |
| | | | | | No |
| | | | | | No |
| | | | | | No |
| | | | | | No |
| | | | | | No |
| | | | | | No |
| | | | | | No |
| | | | | | No |
| | | | | | BLF DR E |
| | | | | | No |
| | | | | | BLF SC |
| | | | | | E |
| | | | | | No |
| | | | | | No |
| | | | | | BLF DR E SC |
| | | | | | |
| | | | | | |

# HYBRID TEA ROSES

## Varieties

| | PLANT DETAILS | | | | BLOOM DETAILS | |
|---|---|---|---|---|---|---|
| | Year of introduction | Height | Resistance to disease | Availability | Size of blooms — Number of petals | Colour Fragrance |

### Reds

The classic colour for a rose, and you will find many fine rich reds in the catalogues — *Alec's Red, National Trust, Royal William* and so on. *Super Star* started the taste for vermilion roses, and some of these merge into the orange group.

| | Year of introduction | Height | Resistance to disease | Availability | Size of blooms — Number of petals | Colour Fragrance |
|---|---|---|---|---|---|---|
| **ABBEYFIELD ROSE** Usually classified as a rosy red, but often distinctly pink. A low-growing H.T for the front of the border. Blooms are not large, but it flowers very freely | 1985 | Short | Good | ★★ | Medium — 30 petals | Rosy red Slightly fragrant |
| **ACE OF HEARTS** An excellent choice for the flower arranger — the cup-shaped blooms last for a long time in water. Growth is upright and the leaves are dark and glossy | 1981 | Medium | Good | ★★ | Large — 30 petals | Dark red Fragrant |
| **ALEC'S RED** This very popular red H.T has been around for many years, but you will have to search to find a better one. The globular flowers are richly perfumed | 1970 | Medium | Good | ★★★★★ | Large — 45 petals | Crimson Very fragrant |
| **ALEXANDER** A rose for hedging or the back of the border. This tall-growing offspring of *Super Star* has its parent's vermilion colouring, and is even more luminescent | 1972 | Tall | Good | ★★★★ | Medium — 20 petals | Orange vermilion Slightly fragrant |
| **BIG CHIEF** A good show-bench variety — the flowers are long-lasting. It is not suitable for bedding — *Big Chief* is not free-flowering and the flowers need protection from rain | 1975 | Medium-tall | Average | ★★ | Large — 30 petals | Deep crimson No fragrance |
| **CHRISTIAN DIOR** Once a favourite — now listed by very few growers. Stems are almost thornless and the flowers bear velvety red petals. Susceptibility to mildew makes it a bad choice | 1959 | Tall | Poor | ★★ | Large — 45 petals | Cherry red No fragrance |
| **CHRYSLER IMPERIAL** This old variety once had a good reputation as an exhibition rose. The blooms are full and pointed. Nowadays the flowers quickly discolour and leaves become mildewed | 1952 | Medium | Poor | ★★ | Large — 45 petals | Deep crimson Very fragrant |
| **DEEP SECRET** The darkest of all red H.Ts — an unusual variety for those who like dark leaves and flowers. Fragrance is outstanding, but don't expect it to brighten up your garden | 1977 | Medium | Good | ★★★ | Large — 40 petals | Deep crimson Very fragrant |
| **DUKE OF WINDSOR** The rose to choose if you want *Super Star* blooms on a compact bush. The stems are very thorny and the blooms are borne in small clusters. Mildew is a problem | 1968 | Short-medium | Poor | ★★★ | Medium — 30 petals | Orange vermilion Very fragrant |
| **ENA HARKNESS** For many years this was Britain's favourite red. The richness and non-fading nature of the flower colour remains excellent, but the blooms continue to hang their heads | 1946 | Short-medium | Average | ★★★ | Large — 30 petals | Crimson scarlet Very fragrant |
| **ERNEST H MORSE** A bright red H.T — the fragrance is good and so is rain-resistance. An excellent choice for bedding or growing as a standard, but you will have to spray against mildew | 1964 | Medium | Average | ★★★★★ | Large — 30 petals | Rich turkey red Very fragrant |
| **FORGOTTEN DREAMS** A prophetic name — this offspring of *Fragrant Cloud* never began to rival the popularity of its illustrious parent. Perhaps there is not enough difference between them | 1980 | Medium | Average | ★★ | Large — 25 petals | Cardinal red Very fragrant |
| **FRAGRANT CLOUD** A star of the rose world for more than 20 years — still regarded as one of the most fragrant post-War varieties. Mildew can be a problem these days | 1964 | Medium | Average | ★★★★★ | Large — 30 petals | Geranium red Very fragrant |
| **INGRID BERGMAN** One of the modern, velvety dark reds — bushes are vigorous, healthy and upright. Free-flowering with abundant leathery foliage — a good bedding and hedging rose | 1986 | Medium | Good | ★★★ | Medium — 35 petals | Deep red Fragrant |
| **JOSEPHINE BRUCE** A sprawling plant which suffers badly from mildew. Flowers are highly scented, large and velvety. Still available, but better velvety reds have recently appeared in the catalogues | 1952 | Short-medium | Poor | ★★★★ | Large — 25 petals | Deep velvety crimson Very fragrant |
| **MADAME LOUIS LAPERRIERE** A recommended deep red H.T with a spicy fragrance. Two outstanding features — blooms from early summer to late autumn and the colour does not fade | 1952 | Short | Average | ★★ | Medium — 45 petals | Dark crimson Very fragrant |
| **MISTER LINCOLN** The velvety red for the back of the border. Several good points — large and fragrant blooms, long stems for cutting, etc. One drawback — flowers open and mature quickly | 1964 | Medium-tall | Average | ★★★ | Large — 35 petals | Dark red Very fragrant |
| **NATIONAL TRUST** An outstanding bedding rose, according to the RNRS. The flowers are bright, multi-petalled and unfading, but they are neither large nor fragrant. A popular variety | 1970 | Short | Good | ★★★★ | Medium — 60 petals | Crimson No fragrance |
| **PAPA MEILLAND** Beautiful blooms — fragrant, large and velvety. The plant itself makes it less desirable — moderate vigour, mildew-prone and rather reluctant to produce flowers | 1963 | Medium | Poor | ★★★ | Large — 35 petals | Dark crimson Very fragrant |
| **PRECIOUS PLATINUM** Brightness is the key feature here — the eye-catching blooms are borne in clusters over a long season. Good for bedding — foliage is glossy and abundant | 1974 | Medium | Good | ★★★★ | Large — 35 petals | Bright crimson Fragrant |

## GARDEN RECORD

| Grown in garden | Year of planting (if known) | Supplier | Performance during the year | Problems during the year | Included in Rose Analysis |
|---|---|---|---|---|---|
| Scarlet | | | Vermilion | Crimson | |
| | | | | | No |
| | | | | | No |
| | | | | | BLF E SC |
| | | | | | BLF DR |
| | | | | | E |
| | | | | | No |
| | | | | | No |
| | | | | | BLF |
| | | | | | No |
| | | | | | SC |
| | | | | | BLF E |
| | | | | | No |
| | | | | | BLF E SC |
| | | | | | No |
| | | | | | SC |
| | | | | | No |
| | | | | | No |
| | | | | | BLF |
| | | | | | SC |
| | | | | | BLF |

# HYBRID TEA ROSES

## Varieties
### Reds continued

| | PLANT DETAILS | | | | BLOOM DETAILS | |
|---|---|---|---|---|---|---|
| | Year of introduction | Height | Resistance to disease | Availability | Size of blooms — Number of petals | Colour — Fragrance |
| **RED DEVIL**<br>Very popular exhibition rose. The blooms are very large and very full, but they will not tolerate rain. A strong-growing bush which flowers freely | 1967 | Medium | Good | ★★★★ | Large — 70 petals | Scarlet; pale scarlet revers — Fragrant |
| **ROYAL WILLIAM**<br>Given the Rose of the Year award for 1987. It is expected to be a star for the 1990s — a fragrant, deep red variety which is strong, healthy and stiff-stemmed | 1987 | Medium | Good | ★★★★ | Medium — 30 petals | Deep red — Fragrant |
| **RUBY WEDDING**<br>An excellent cut flower — the modest-sized blooms are borne stiffly erect on straight stems. There are better reds to choose from for bedding | 1979 | Short | Average | ★★★ | Medium — 30 petals | Ruby red — Slightly fragrant |
| **SUPER STAR**<br>Many words have been used to describe the appearance of the blooms — 'fluorescent', 'luminescent' etc. It has been a great star, of course, but no longer a super star | 1960 | Medium-tall | Poor | ★★★★ | Medium — 35 petals | Orange vermilion — Fragrant |
| | | | | | | |
| | | | | | | |

## Lilacs

The search for the blue rose goes on — the listed 'blues' are really lilacs and mauves. Sometimes attractive, but more often these blooms look dull and faded. You will find very few in the catalogues.

| | | | | | | |
|---|---|---|---|---|---|---|
| **BLUE MOON**<br>Generally agreed to be the best of the 'blue' roses. Flowers have a classic shape and the fragrance is strong and unusual. Good for cutting | 1964 | Medium | Average | ★★★★★ | Medium — 35 petals | Silvery lilac — Very fragrant |
| **BLUE PARFUM**<br>Blooms are larger but less fragrant than *Blue Moon*. Growth is vigorous and upright — *Blue Parfum* is recommended for cutting. You will find this one in few catalogues | 1978 | Medium | Average | ★★ | Large — 25 petals | Mauve — Fragrant |
| | | | | | | |

## Bi-colours & Stripes

Bi-colours bear petals on which the colour of the outside is distinctly different from the inside hue. They can be very colourful, but not many have become popular. Striped varieties are even less popular.

| | | | | | | |
|---|---|---|---|---|---|---|
| **BOBBY CHARLTON**<br>Good for exhibiting — not too good for garden display. The flowers have the size and shape for winning prizes, but flowering begins late and not many blooms are produced | 1974 | Medium | Poor | ★★ | Large — 35 petals | Deep pink; silver reverse — Fragrant |
| **GAY GORDONS**<br>Garish blooms on a compact low-growing bush. Not a popular variety — the flowers appear in great profusion but the leaves suffer badly from black spot | 1969 | Short | Poor | ★★ | Medium — 25 petals | Red and orange yellow revers — Slightly fragra |
| **HARRY WHEATCROFT**<br>This sport of *Piccadilly* is the only striped H.T you are likely to find. The bushes are compact and free-flowering — the flowers are pointed and brightly striped | 1963 | Medium | Poor | ★★★ | Large — 25 petals | Scarlet, striped yello — Slightly fragra |
| **KRONENBOURG**<br>A winner if it had lived up to its promise. Unfortunately the young blooms discolour badly with age and this sport sometimes reverts back to its parent, the legendary *Peace* | 1965 | Tall | Average | ★★ | Large — 45 petals | Crimson; old gold reverse — Slightly fragra |
| **MY CHOICE**<br>This one was expected to become a winner. A large and very fragrant bi-colour with strong and healthy growth was novel, but it failed to appeal | 1958 | Medium | Good | ★★ | Large — 35 petals | Pink; yellow revers — Very fragran |
| **PICCADILLY**<br>Even after 30 years this variety remains the best-selling bi-colour. Disease has become a problem but many good points remain — early and free-flowering plus attractive foliage | 1959 | Short-medium | Poor | ★★★★★ | Medium — 25 petals | Scarlet; pale yellow revers — Slightly fragra |
| **ROSE GAUJARD**<br>A good bedding rose if you like bi-colours. This old favourite has healthy growth and the blooms are borne very freely. It grows well under poor conditions | 1958 | Medium-tall | Good | ★★★★ | Large — 30 petals | Rose red; silver reverse — Slightly fragra |
| **ROSY CHEEKS**<br>Some experts are puzzled why this bi-colour is not a best-seller. The fragrant blooms are very large and the bushes are healthy but the public has said no | 1976 | Short-medium | Good | ★★★ | Large — 30 petals | Red; pale yellow revers — |
| **TENERIFE**<br>Two famous parents — it is fragrant like *Fragrant Cloud* and a bi-colour like *Piccadilly*. Unfortunately it has its problems — susceptibility to disease is the worst | 1972 | Medium | Poor | ★★ | Large — 35 petals | Coral salmon peach revers — Very fragran |
| | | | | | | |

| GARDEN RECORD | | | | | Included in Rose Analysis |
|---|---|---|---|---|---|
| Grown in garden | Year of planting (if known) | Supplier | Performance during the year | Problems during the year | |
| | | | | | E |
| | | | | | N |
| | | | | | No |
| | | | | | BLF E |
| | | | | | |
| | | | | | |

Lilac    Mauve

| | | | | | |
|---|---|---|---|---|---|
| | | | | | SC |
| | | | | | No |
| | | | | | |

Bi-colour    Bi-colour    Stripes

| | | | | | |
|---|---|---|---|---|---|
| | | | | | No |
| | | | | | No |
| | | | | | No |
| | | | | | No |
| | | | | | No |
| | | | | | BLF |
| | | | | | BLF DR E |
| | | | | | No |
| | | | | | No |
| | | | | | |

VARIETIES

# Hybrid Teas~ the top sellers

Listed here are the 20 varieties which professional rose growers consider to be their most popular roses. The presence of a rose on this page does not mean that it is highly recommended by the experts, but it does reflect widespread appeal to gardeners throughout the country.

*Royal William*

*Polar Star*

*Fragrant Cloud*

*Whisky Mac*

*Peace*

*Silver Jubilee*

*Piccadilly*

*Alec's Red*

Just Joey

Pascali

Blue Moon

Grandpa Dickson

Blessings

Ernest H Morse

Doris Tysterman

Lovers' Meeting

Prima Ballerina

Super Star

King's Ransom

Alexander

VARIETIES

# FLORIBUNDA ROSES

| Varieties | PLANT DETAILS | | | | BLOOM DETAILS | |
|---|---|---|---|---|---|---|
| | Year of introduction | Height | Resistance to disease | Availability | Size of blooms — Number of petals | Colour — Fragrance |
| **Whites & Creams** | Whites and creams are not popular Floribunda colours, and pure whites are rar *Iceberg* is sometimes and *Margaret Merril* is always tinged with pink. *Bianco* is occasionally creamy rather than white. | | | | | |
| **BIANCO** A low and spreading Patio variety — choose it where space is a problem. The clusters are large and freely produced, each flower a white or creamy white rosette | 1983 | Short | Average | ★★ | Small — 25 petals | White — No fragranc |
| **CHANELLE** Peaches and cream, according to some books, but the cream definitely predominates. A thoroughly reliable variety, with healthy leaves and lots of flowers | 1958 | Medium | Good | ★★ | Medium — 20 petals | Cream, flush buff — Fragrant |
| **ICEBERG** The unchallenged queen of white Floribundas. If pruned lightly the bush is covered with large clusters of white blooms throughout the season. Good for hedging | 1958 | Medium-tall | Poor | ★★★★★ | Medium — 25 petals | White — Slightly fragrant |
| **MARGARET MERRIL** The white to choose if you want fragrance. The blooms are shapelier than the other whites, but flowering is less free and the clusters bear fewer blooms | 1978 | Medium | Average | ★★★★★ | Medium — 30 petals | Pearly whit — Very fragra |
| | | | | | | |
| **Yellows** | There are many yellow Floribundas, and these are often pure yellows without blend or veins of other colours. Favourites here are *Allgold*, *Korresia* and *Mountbatten*. Some fade in the sun (e.g *Arthur Bell* and *Sunsilk*) but most are colour-fast. | | | | | |
| **ALLGOLD** An old variety still to be found in most catalogues. A compact bush which starts to flower early and goes on until late autumn. Foliage may be sparse | 1956 | Short | Good | ★★★★ | Small — 20 petals | Buttercup yellow — Slightly fragr |
| **AMBER QUEEN** Rose of the Year in 1984. Neat and compact — this variety makes an excellent bedding rose. Foliage is abundant and the cup-shaped blooms are large | 1984 | Short | Good | ★★★★ | Large — 40 petals | Amber yello — Fragrant |
| **ANNE HARKNESS** A taller-than-average variety recommended for flower arranging, hedging and exhibiting. Flowering begins late, but there is a fine display in mid and late season | 1980 | Medium-tall | Good | ★★★ | Medium — 25 petals | Apricot yello — Slightly fragrant |
| **ARD'S BEAUTY** A supreme award winner which has not reached the best-seller lists. It has many good points — large fragrant flowers, healthy foliage etc, but nothing extraordinary | 1986 | Medium | Good | ★★ | Large — 20 petals | Canary yello — Fragrant |
| **ARTHUR BELL** A tall and upright bush with outstandingly fragrant flowers and excellent resistance to disease. The blooms stand up to rain but they do fade with age | 1965 | Medium-tall | Good | ★★★★ | Large — 20 petals | Golden yello — Very fragran |
| **BABY BIO** One of the best of the dwarf yellows — its popularity has steadily increased. The flowers are remarkably large and full for such a small bush. Flowers freely all season | 1977 | Short | Good | ★★★ | Large — 40 petals | Golden yelle — Slightly fragrant |
| **BRIGHT SMILE** An excellent variety, hampered only by a shortage of petals. This drawback is overcome by the abundance of blooms. Foliage is plentiful and flowering starts early | 1980 | Short | Good | ★★★ | Medium — 15 petals | Yellow — Slightly fragrant |
| **BURMA STAR** Tall and stately with blooms which look more like an H.T than a typical Floribunda. This variety has never become popular and is missing from most catalogues | 1974 | Tall | Good | ★★ | Large — 20 petals | Apricot yello — Slightly fragrant |
| **HONEYMOON** Each cluster bears rosette-shaped blooms with lots of petals and little scent. It has its problems — the colour tends to fade and there are gaps between flushes | 1959 | Medium | Good | ★★ | Medium — 40 petals | Canary yello — Slightly fragrant |
| **KORRESIA** A popular yellow — it provides larger and more fragrant blooms than *Allgold*. The trusses bear many blooms and the colour is unfading. A good choice | 1974 | Short-medium | Good | ★★★★ | Large — 35 petals | Bright yello — Fragrant |
| **MOUNTBATTEN** One of the tall-growing stars of the 1980s. The upright stems bear semi-evergreen leaves and the trusses carry large, sweet-smelling flowers. Give the bushes room | 1982 | Tall | Good | ★★★★★ | Large — 45 petals | Mimosa yell — Fragrant |

The Floribundas began in 1924 with *Else Poulsen,* a cross between a Polyantha and a Hybrid Tea. The group is now second only to the Hybrid Teas in popularity. The Floribunda bears its flowers in clusters or trusses, and several blooms open at the same time in each truss. These varieties are unrivalled for providing colourful, reliable and long-lasting bedding display, but in general the flower form is inferior to that of the Hybrid Tea. Patio types (see page 2) have become popular. The World Federation of Rose Societies prefers the name 'Cluster-flowered Roses' but catalogues still use the traditional term.

**VARIETIES**

| | GARDEN RECORD | | | | Included in Rose Analysis |
|---|---|---|---|---|---|
| own in rden | Year of planting (if known) | Supplier | Performance during the year | Problems during the year | |
| White | | Creamy white | | Ivory | |
| | | | | | No |
| | | | | | No |
| | | | | | BCF E SH |
| | | | | | BCF SC |
| | | | | | |
| Primrose yellow | Canary yellow | | Golden yellow | Buttercup yellow | |
| | | | | | BCF |
| | | | | | BCF N |
| | | | | | BCF E |
| | | | | | No |
| | | | | | BCF |
| | | | | | No |
| | | | | | No |
| | | | | | No |
| | | | | | No |
| | | | | | BCF DR |
| | | | | | BCF SH |

# FLORIBUNDA ROSES

## Varieties
### Yellows continued

### Oranges & Blends

A popular colour for Floribundas, ranging from the near-yellow of *Glenfiddich* to the near-red of *Orange Sensation*. Blends (see page 10 for definition) come in many shades and forms. The Hand-painted group (see page 30) are treated separately.

| | PLANT DETAILS | | | | BLOOM DETAILS | |
|---|---|---|---|---|---|---|
| | Year of introduction | Height | Resistance to disease | Availability | Size of blooms — Number of petals | Colour — Fragrance |
| **PRINCESS ALICE** Differs from most other healthy yellows by having the blooms attractively arranged in each truss. Growth is upright and it can be quite tall. Showy, but not a top seller | 1985 | Medium-tall | Good | ★★ | Medium — 25 petals | Yellow — Slightly fragrant |
| **SUNSILK** Large H.T-type blooms are the most distinctive feature of this variety. The autumn display is outstanding — midsummer flowers tend to fade with age. Rust can be a problem | 1974 | Medium | Average | ★★ | Large — 35 petals | Lemon yellow — Slightly fragrant |
| **ANNA FORD** A small Floribunda — classed as a Miniature in some catalogues. Popular, and rightly so. Compact bushes are covered with reddish blooms which fade with age | 1980 | Very short | Good | ★★★ | Small — 20 petals | Deep orange yellow eye — Slightly fragra |
| **DAME OF SARK** Useful for hedging or bedding, but not as a specimen plant. The blooms are bright, but the petals are loose and untidy. Health and rain resistance are good | 1976 | Medium | Good | ★★ | Large — 35 petals | Golden yello flushed scarl — Slightly fragra |
| **ELIZABETH OF GLAMIS** Such a wonderful rose in its time — large, flat blooms in wide-spreading trusses. There are too many problems these days — it will not tolerate cold or wet conditions | 1964 | Medium | Poor | ★★★★★ | Large — 35 petals | Orange salm — Fragrant |
| **ESCAPADE** Easily recognised — a white-centred ring of lilac petals surrounding a group of yellow stamens. The scented blooms are large and flat and the leaves are plentiful | 1967 | Medium | Average | ★★ | Large — 10 petals | Rosy lilac; white eye — Fragrant |
| **FRAGRANT DELIGHT** This rose won the prestigious James Mason award in 1988. Blooms are large and trusses are small — flower form and fragrance are outstanding | 1978 | Short-medium | Good | ★★★★ | Large — 20 petals | Coppery salm yellow at bas — Very fragran |
| **GERALDINE** Now for something different — a rose with the colour of orange peel. The unusual colour makes it a good specimen rose, but it is also recommended for cutting and exhibiting | 1983 | Medium | Good | ★★★ | Medium — 20 petals | Orange — Slightly fragrant |
| **GLENFIDDICH** A popular orange, noted for the warm colour of its flowers and the large size of its trusses. Flower continuity is excellent and so is the shape of the blooms | 1976 | Medium | Good | ★★★★ | Medium — 25 petals | Golden amb — Slightly fragrant |
| **HANNAH GORDON** An unusual flower which is rather similar to the popular climber *Handel*. The white petals have a deep pink rim and the blooms are large. Different, but not a top seller | 1983 | Medium | Average | ★★ | Large — 30 petals | White, edge dark pink — Slightly fragra |
| **ICED GINGER** There are better bedding roses — growth is rather lanky and it is not always free-flowering. For cutting, however, it has few rivals. The blooms last remarkably well in water | 1971 | Medium | Good | ★★★ | Large — 45 petals | Ivory, tinted coppery pin — Fragrant |
| **ORANGE SENSATION** This Floribunda has its good points — large trusses, vivid colour, good scent etc. It also has its problems — dull foliage, mildew and a rather late start to flowering | 1960 | Short-medium | Poor | ★★★★ | Medium — 25 petals | Light vermilion — Fragrant |
| **ORANGEADE** Petals are few, but flowers are plentiful if you dead-head regularly. Included in the 'orange' group, but the mature blooms are as dark as the vermilion 'reds' | 1959 | Medium | Poor | ★★ | Medium — 10 petals | Light vermilion — Slightly fragra |
| **PEEK A BOO** Patio Rose or Miniature — it depends on which catalogue you consult. Comes to flower early in the season — useful in a rockery. With age the petals turn pink | 1981 | Very short | Average | ★★★★ | Small — 20 petals | Apricot — Slightly fragrant |
| **RED GOLD** A bright Floribunda which has been around for many years — the young flowers are red and gold. Useful for bedding and exhibiting, but mildew is a problem | 1967 | Medium | Poor | ★★ | Medium — 25 petals | Golden yello edged cherry — Slightly fragra |
| **SHEILA'S PERFUME** How could this one fail to be a top seller ... but it has. Classic H.T shape, healthy growth, strongly scented, bushy form, bright colouring etc. You can't predict a winner | 1985 | Short-medium | Good | ★★★ | Large — 20 petals | Yellow, edged red — Very fragra |
| **SOUTHAMPTON** Use it for a large bed, border or hedge. A popular choice — the marmalade-coloured blooms have a ruffled edge and the rather tall and upright plants pose no problems | 1971 | Medium-tall | Good | ★★★★ | Large — 25 petals | Apricot oran flushed scar — Slightly fragra |
| **STARGAZER** A knee-high bush with single blooms was never going to be popular, and so *Stargazer* has disappeared from most catalogues. Still worth considering | 1977 | Very short | Good | ★★ | Medium — 5 petals | Orange scarl golden eye — Slightly fragra |

| Grown in garden | Year of planting (if known) | Supplier | Performance during the year | Problems during the year | Included in Rose Analysis |
|---|---|---|---|---|---|
| | | | | | N |
| | | | | | No |
| | | | | | |
| | | | | | |

🌹 Apricot   🌹 Salmon   🌹 Peach   🌹 Tangerine   🌹 Blend

| | | | | | |
|---|---|---|---|---|---|
| | | | | | No |
| | | | | | No |
| | | | | | BCF |
| | | | | | BCF |
| | | | | | BCF |
| | | | | | No |
| | | | | | BCF |
| | | | | | No |
| | | | | | No |
| | | | | | No |
| | | | | | No |
| | | | | | No |
| | | | | | No |
| | | | | | No |
| | | | | | BCF DR |
| | | | | | No |

VARIETIES

# FLORIBUNDA ROSES

## Varieties
### Oranges & Blends continued

| | PLANT DETAILS | | | | BLOOM DETAILS | |
|---|---|---|---|---|---|---|
| | Year of introduction | Height | Resistance to disease | Availability | Size of blooms — Number of petals | Colour Fragrance |
| **SWEET DREAM**<br>Rose of the Year in 1988. This Patio Rose has cushion-like growth — foliage is abundant. The peachy blooms are rain- and fade-resistant — a good choice for tub or edging | 1988 | Short | Good | ★★★★ | Medium — 35 petals | Apricot — Fragrant |
| **SWEET MAGIC**<br>Like *Sweet Dream*, a winner of the Rose of the Year award. The flowers are smaller and less full, opening wide to reveal the glowing orange and yellow hues | 1987 | Short | Good | ★★★★ | Small — 15 petals | Orange, blended gold — Fragrant |
| **WOBURN ABBEY**<br>The attractive colour of the blooms keeps this old favourite in the catalogues, but you can do better these days. It is prone to all the diseases, and the flowers are untidy | 1962 | Medium | Poor | ★★★ | Medium — 25 petals | Coppery orange shaded gold — Fragrant |
| | | | | | | |
| | | | | | | |

## Pinks

The range of pink Floribundas is somewhat limited compared to the pink H.Ts, but the whole span of hues is covered. This ranges from the near-whites (*Gentle Touch* and *English Miss*) to the near-oranges such as *Tip Top* and *Wishing*.

| | Year of introduction | Height | Resistance to disease | Availability | Size of blooms — Number of petals | Colour Fragrance |
|---|---|---|---|---|---|---|
| **ANISLEY DICKSON**<br>This bushy variety won the RNRS supreme award in 1984, but has failed to gain the popularity which was expected. Maybe it's the complex name — even the RNRS got it wrong! | 1985 | Medium | Good | ★★★ | Large — 30 petals | Salmon pink — Slightly fragrant |
| **CITY OF LEEDS**<br>Floral abundance makes this a popular variety. Trusses are large, flowers are plentiful and the flowering season is long. Reliable, but flowers spot after heavy rain | 1966 | Medium | Average | ★★★ | Medium — 20 petals | Salmon pink — Slightly fragrant |
| **DEAREST**<br>Once the top-selling pink Floribunda. The trusses are crowded with large camellia-like blooms. There are two drawbacks — disease and lack of rain resistance | 1960 | Short-medium | Poor | ★★★★ | Large — 30 petals | Salmon pink — Fragrant |
| **ENGLISH MISS**<br>A child of *Dearest*, but healthier and much more rain-resistant. A good choice — there is a strong spicy scent and there is only a short interval between flushes | 1978 | Short-medium | Good | ★★★ | Medium — 35 petals | Silver pink, edged deeper pink — Very fragrant |
| **GENTLE TOUCH**<br>Rose of the Year in 1986. Another Patio Rose which has walked off with top honours. Young blooms have a classic H.T shape and the trusses bear 20 blooms or more | 1986 | Very short | Average | ★★★★ | Small — 15 petals | Pale pink — Slightly fragrant |
| **PADDY McGREDY**<br>An old favourite with large blooms on a small bush. Bloom size and shape are its attraction — against it are disease, rain damage, delays between flushes and colour-fading | 1962 | Short | Poor | ★★★ | Large — 35 petals | Deep rose pink — Slightly fragrant |
| **PINK PARFAIT**<br>The catalogues rightly sing the praises of this pink and cream favourite. Blooming is almost continuous and the rain-resistant flowers are excellent for cutting | 1960 | Medium | Good | ★★★ | Medium — 20 petals | Pink; cream at base — No fragrance |
| **QUEEN ELIZABETH**<br>One of the world's great roses. A little surprising, perhaps, as it is too tall for bedding in small gardens. An excellent hedging or specimen plant with all its well-known virtues still intact | 1955 | Tall | Good | ★★★★★ | Large — 35 petals | Light pink — Slightly fragrant |
| **SCENTED AIR**<br>Fragrance is the notable feature here — neither colour nor flower form is anything special. Flowers, trusses and leaves are large and healthy — a reliable bedding rose | 1965 | Medium | Good | ★★ | Large — 20 petals | Deep salmon pink — Very fragrant |
| **SEXY REXY**<br>A new pink with all the virtues apart from fragrance. Growth is bushy and the trusses bear an exceptional number of blooms. It is recommended for cutting and bedding | 1985 | Medium | Good | ★★ | Large — 40 petals | Medium pink — Slightly fragrant |
| **SHONA**<br>A run-of-the-mill pink Floribunda — noted for its neat growth habit and dense foliage. It makes a reliable low hedge, but there are better pinks for bedding | 1982 | Short-medium | Average | ★★ | Medium — 20 petals | Coral pink — Slightly fragrant |
| **TIP TOP**<br>An old favourite, but still the usual choice when a low-growing pink Floribunda is required. Both the flowering season and freedom of flowering are exceptional | 1963 | Very short | Poor | ★★★★ | Medium — 20 petals | Salmon pink — Slightly fragrant |
| **WISHING**<br>The standard catalogue description provides a clear picture — the colour is richer than its parent *Silver Jubilee*. The bush is smaller, and the blooms are borne in clusters | 1985 | Short-medium | Good | ★★ | Medium — 35 petals | Salmon pink, shaded peach — Slightly fragrant |
| | | | | | | |
| | | | | | | |

| | | GARDEN RECORD | | | | Included in Rose Analysis |
|---|---|---|---|---|---|---|
| Grown in garden | Year of planting (if known) | Supplier | Performance during the year | | Problems during the year | |
| | | | | | | No |
| | | | | | | No |
| | | | | | | No |
| | | | | | | |
| | | | | | | |

Pink    Shell pink    Rose pink    Carmine rose

| | | | | | |
|---|---|---|---|---|---|
| | | | | | N |
| | | | | | BCF |
| | | | | | BCF |
| | | | | | No |
| | | | | | N |
| | | | | | No |
| | | | | | BCF |
| | | | | | BCF DR SH |
| | | | | | No |
| | | | | | No |
| | | | | | No |
| | | | | | No |
| | | | | | No |
| | | | | | |
| | | | | | |

VARIETIES

# FLORIBUNDA ROSES

## Varieties

| | PLANT DETAILS | | | | BLOOM DETAILS | |
|---|---|---|---|---|---|---|
| | Year of introduction | Height | Resistance to disease | Availability | Size of blooms — Number of petals | Colour — Fragrance |

### Reds

The reds make up the largest Floribunda colour group, and the choice is truly impressive. There are the vivid ones (*Topsi*, *Evelyn Fison*, *Chorus* etc) and the quiet ones like *Memento*. On either side of the true reds are the near-orange (e.g *Disco Dancer*) and the near-pink varieties like *Rosemary Rose*.

| Variety | Year of introduction | Height | Resistance to disease | Availability | Size of blooms — Number of petals | Colour — Fragrance |
|---|---|---|---|---|---|---|
| **ANNE COCKER**<br>The flowers are small and they have no scent. This variety has its points, though — the number of blooms in the truss is extraordinary and so is their life in water | 1971 | Medium-tall | Average | ★★ | Small<br>—<br>35 petals | Vermilion<br>—<br>No fragrance |
| **BEAUTIFUL BRITAIN**<br>Rose of the Year in 1983 — the unusual tomato colour caught the eye of the judges. So did the abundant foliage, large trusses and free-flowering habit | 1983 | Short-medium | Good | ★★★★ | Medium<br>—<br>20 petals | Tomato red<br>—<br>Slightly fragrant |
| **BOYS' BRIGADE**<br>It is difficult for a small, semi-double flower to become popular. This Patio Rose makes a change, but lacks the flower form and petallage required of a top seller | 1983 | Short | Average | ★★ | Small<br>—<br>10 petals | Red; cream eye<br>—<br>No fragrance |
| **CHORUS**<br>One of the brightest red Floribundas. The blooms are large and it has an excellent health record. It is recommended for bedding and exhibiting, but has not become popular | 1975 | Medium | Good | ★★ | Large<br>—<br>35 petals | Crimson<br>—<br>Slightly fragrant |
| **CITY OF BELFAST**<br>A good choice for the small garden where a bright splash of red is required. Disease is not a problem, but die-back can be a nuisance | 1968 | Short-medium | Good | ★★ | Small<br>—<br>35 petals | Scarlet<br>—<br>No fragrance |
| **DISCO DANCER**<br>Orange or red — it is hard to decide. Trusses are crowded. The colour is vivid and luminescent — surrounding plants can look dull. A good choice for a low hedge | 1984 | Medium | Good | ★★ | Medium<br>—<br>25 petals | Orange scarlet<br>—<br>Slightly fragrant |
| **EUROPEANA**<br>The trusses of large, open flowers bow their heads in wet weather — close planting is needed to provide support. Foliage is also distinctive — reddish purple when young | 1963 | Medium | Poor | ★★ | Medium<br>—<br>40 petals | Dark red<br>—<br>Slightly fragrant |
| **EVELYN FISON**<br>She has been around for a long time, but *Evelyn Fison* remains a thoroughly reliable choice. Colour is quite vivid, and neither sun nor rain affects the blooms | 1962 | Short-medium | Average | ★★★★★ | Medium<br>—<br>30 petals | Bright scarlet<br>—<br>Slightly fragrant |
| **EYE PAINT**<br>A single row of petals — flowers are small but trusses are huge. The bushes are tall with a Shrub Rose look. Use for hedging or planting in the shrub border | 1976 | Tall | Average | ★★ | Small<br>—<br>7 petals | Scarlet; white eye<br>—<br>No fragrance |
| **FRENSHAM**<br>Our most popular red Floribunda for many years after World War II. Foliage is plentiful and the trusses are large. There are healthier reds these days for bedding | 1946 | Tall | Poor | ★★ | Medium<br>—<br>15 petals | Deep crimson<br>—<br>No fragrance |
| **KORONA**<br>Once the No.1 vermilion Floribunda — now largely ignored when choosing plants for the garden. Still free-flowering and rain-resistant, *Korona* these days is no longer reliable | 1954 | Medium | Average | ★★ | Medium<br>—<br>20 petals | Orange scarlet<br>—<br>Slightly fragrant |
| **LILLI MARLENE**<br>Disease can be a problem, but this variety remains popular because it is tolerant of poor conditions and bears velvety, dark red blooms. Rounded bushes bear abundant foliage | 1959 | Medium | Poor | ★★★★ | Medium<br>—<br>25 petals | Deep crimson<br>—<br>Slightly fragrant |
| **MARLENA**<br>A popular edging rose, growing about 20 in. high. The small bushes bear a mass of bright red flowers in large clusters. Leafy and compact for the front of the border | 1964 | Short | Good | ★★ | Medium<br>—<br>20 petals | Crimson<br>—<br>No fragrance |
| **MEMENTO**<br>Flowers are abundant throughout the season — each bloom is a flat rosette. Hardy and resistant to rain — a sound choice for bedding and cutting. Growth is upright | 1978 | Medium | Average | ★★ | Medium<br>—<br>25 petals | Salmon vermilion<br>—<br>Slightly fragrant |
| **METEOR**<br>A small Floribunda which first appeared many years ago. Still a good choice — there is a long flowering season and health remains good. Use for edging or the front of the border | 1958 | Short | Good | ★★ | Medium<br>—<br>40 petals | Orange scarlet<br>—<br>No fragrance |
| **PICCOLO**<br>This variety has brought orange-red to the Patio Rose group. Rather larger than other Patio types, with blooms which are also large for this group. Nice, but not outstanding | 1983 | Short | Good | ★★★ | Medium<br>—<br>20 petals | Coral red<br>—<br>No fragrance |
| **PILLAR BOX**<br>Well-named — it is tall, upright and clothed in red when in full flower. One for the back of the border, like its parent *Alexander*. Also good for hedging | 1981 | Tall | Good | ★★ | Large<br>—<br>20 petals | Vermilion<br>—<br>Slightly fragrant |
| **ROB ROY**<br>H.T-shaped blooms, as bright as any red you will find. A hardy rose which has not become popular, despite its vivid colour. Disease can be a problem | 1971 | Medium-tall | Poor | ★★★ | Large<br>—<br>20 petals | Bright crimson<br>—<br>Slightly fragrant |
| **ROSEMARY ROSE**<br>The large, camellia-like blooms give this rose an old-fashioned look. Growth is spreading and foliage is bronze red — a good out-of-the-ordinary choice | 1955 | Short-medium | Poor | ★★ | Large<br>—<br>35 petals | Rosy red<br>—<br>Fragrant |
| **SCARLET QUEEN ELIZABETH**<br>Tall, colourful and healthy, this offspring is not really close to its parent. The blooms are loose and open and flowers are sometimes rather sparse and hidden in the foliage | 1963 | Tall | Good | ★★★ | Medium<br>—<br>25 petals | Orange scarlet<br>—<br>Slightly fragrant |

| GARDEN RECORD | | | | | Included in Rose Analysis |
|---|---|---|---|---|---|
| Grown in garden | Year of planting (if known) | Supplier | Performance during the year | Problems during the year | |
| | | 🌹 Vermilion | 🌹 Scarlet | 🌹 Crimson | |
| | | | | | No |
| | | | | | No |
| | | | | | No |
| | | | | | No |
| | | | | | No |
| | | | | | No |
| | | | | | No |
| | | | | | BCF |
| | | | | | BCF |
| | | | | | No |
| | | | | | No |
| | | | | | BCF |
| | | | | | No |
| | | | | | No |
| | | | | | No |
| | | | | | No |
| | | | | | No |
| | | | | | No |
| | | | | | No |

VARIETIES

## Varieties

# FLORIBUNDA ROSES

### Reds continued

| | PLANT DETAILS | | | | BLOOM DETAILS | |
| --- | --- | --- | --- | --- | --- | --- |
| | Year of introduction | Height | Resistance to disease | Availability | Size of blooms — Number of petals | Colour — Fragrance |
| **THE TIMES ROSE**<br>Another modern red of average height — this one won the supreme award of the RNRS. Clusters are large, the dark green foliage is abundant and the shape ideal for bedding | 1984 | Medium | Good | ★★ | Large — 30 petals | Blood red — Slightly fragrant |
| **TOPSI**<br>A Patio Rose with many good points. The flowers are vivid and non-fading, the period of flowering is prolonged and the flushes repeat in quick succession. Mildew is a problem | 1972 | Very short | Poor | ★★★ | Medium — 10 petals | Bright vermilion — No fragrance |
| **TRUMPETER**<br>Short — but too tall to be a Patio Rose. Bright, like *Topsi*, but it has many more petals and better disease resistance. The trusses are very large | 1978 | Short | Good | ★★★ | Medium — 35 petals | Bright vermilion — Slightly fragrant |
| **WARRIOR**<br>The colour is a deeper red than the vermilion of *Trumpeter*, but many other features of the two varieties are quite similar. Most gardeners choose *Trumpeter* rather than *Warrior* | 1978 | Short | Good | ★★ | Medium — 30 petals | Scarlet — Slightly fragrant |
| | | | | | | |
| | | | | | | |

### Hand-painted

Silvery petals with red or pink blotched and/or feathered over the surface. There is a white eye at the base. Both *Marlena* and *Evelyn Fison* were amongst the ancestors of *Picasso*, the original Hand-painted variety introduced by McGredy.

| | | | | | | |
| --- | --- | --- | --- | --- | --- | --- |
| **LAUGHTER LINES**<br>One of the newer Hand-painted varieties — a Gold Medal winner in 1984. Hardy, healthy and with blooms which are a kaleidoscope of colour. Flowering starts early | 1984 | Medium | Good | ★★ | Medium — 15 petals | Pink and white veined red — Slightly fragrant |
| **MATANGI**<br>Classed as Hand-painted (*Picasso* is a parent) but with a rather plain face for this group. The central area of the bloom has white blotches — there is no veining. A reliable variety | 1974 | Medium | Good | ★★★ | Medium — 25 petals | Vermilion; white eye silver reverse — Slightly fragrant |
| **PICASSO**<br>The first of the Hand-painted roses — pink with irregular splashes of red. Prune lightly. Newer varieties are thought to be better — more flowers and brighter colours | 1971 | Short-medium | Poor | ★★ | Medium — 25 petals | Deep pink, blotched red; silver reverse — No fragrance |
| **REGENSBERG**<br>A Patio variety with surprisingly large flowers. These blooms open flat to reveal a complex blend of pink and white. A must for the Hand-painted fan | 1979 | Short | Good | ★★★ | Large — 20 petals | Pale pink and white — Fragrant |
| **SUE LAWLEY**<br>The variety to buy for pronounced "crayoning" of the petals. Trusses bear several blooms. A useful rose for bedding and cutting — taller but less fragrant than *Regensberg* | 1980 | Medium | Average | ★★ | Large — 20 petals | Carmine, pink and white — Slightly fragrant |
| | | | | | | |

### Miscellaneous

Both green and 'blue' Floribundas occur, but they are limited to just one or two varieties. Bi-colours are less rare, but they are still an extremely unusual colour type. Multi-coloured Floribundas have a range of colours in the truss — *Masquerade* is the only one you are likely to see.

| | | | | | | |
| --- | --- | --- | --- | --- | --- | --- |
| **GOLDEN SLIPPERS**<br>A bi-coloured Floribunda — such types are unusual but *Golden Slippers* has not become popular. It is a delicate variety — growth is slight and it is unreliable | 1961 | Short | Good | ★★ | Medium — 20 petals | Rich orange; gold yellow reverse — Fragrant |
| **GREENSLEEVES**<br>The light pink buds change to green as the flowers open. This one is strictly for the flower arranger or the curio collector — too leggy for garden display | 1980 | Medium | Poor | ★★ | Large — 15 petals | Chartreuse green — No fragrance |
| **MASQUERADE**<br>The ever-popular multi-coloured rose for hedging and general garden display. Each large truss bears a medley of colours — dead-head regularly. Each bloom is rather small | 1949 | Medium-tall | Average | ★★★ | Medium — 15 petals | Yellow, changing pink and red — Slightly fragrant |
| **SEA PEARL**<br>Colourful blooms on rather tall, upright bushes. The flowers are shapely when young and the blend of pink, peach and yellow can be attractive. They are spotted by rain | 1964 | Medium-tall | Good | ★★ | Large — 25 petals | Pink; yellow reverse — Slightly fragrant |
| **SHOCKING BLUE**<br>An excellent choice for the flower arranger — H.T-shaped blooms in an unusual colour. Not blue, of course — it's mauve or deep lilac. The fragrance is outstanding | 1974 | Medium | Good | ★★ | Large — 30 petals | Lilac mauve — Very fragrant |
| | | | | | | |
| | | | | | | |

| GARDEN RECORD | | | | | Included in Rose Analysis |
|---|---|---|---|---|---|
| Grown in garden | Year of planting (if known) | Supplier | Performance during the year | Problems during the year | |
| | | | | | N |
| | | | | | No |
| | | | | | BCF |
| | | | | | No |
| | | | | | |
| | | | | | |

Hand-painted

| | | | | | |
|---|---|---|---|---|---|
| | | | | | No |
| | | | | | BCF |
| | | | | | No |
| | | | | | No |
| | | | | | No |
| | | | | | |

Bi-colour    Green    Lilac    Multi-colour

| | | | | | |
|---|---|---|---|---|---|
| | | | | | No |
| | | | | | No |
| | | | | | BCF |
| | | | | | No |
| | | | | | No |
| | | | | | |
| | | | | | |

VARIETIES

# Floribundas~ the top sellers

Listed here are the 20 varieties which professional rose growers consider to be their most popular roses. The presence of a rose on this page does not mean that it is highly recommended by the experts, but it does reflect widespread appeal to gardeners throughout the country.

*Iceberg*

*Queen Elizabeth*

*Mountbatten*

*Evelyn Fison*

*Glenfiddich*

*Elizabeth of Glamis*

*Margaret Merril*

*Amber Queen*

**Fragrant Delight**

**Dearest**

**Korresia**

**Sweet Dream**

**Arthur Bell**

**Trumpeter**

**Lilli Marlene**

**Tip Top**

**Orange Sensation**

**Beautiful Britain**

**Allgold**

**Masquerade**

VARIETIES

# MINIATURES

Miniatures were popular in mid-Victorian times but they mysteriously disappeared. A single pot was seen in Switzerland in 1918 and was used for hybridisation, and so the modern Miniature story began. With this class both leaves and flowers are scaled-down versions of standard-sized ones. Short varieties grow up to 9 in. high and tall Miniatures reach 18 in. A small bloom is less than an inch — a large one is about 2 in. across. Miniatures can be used for edging beds, growing in tubs and rockeries or taking indoors as temporary pot plants. They are still the Cinderella of the rose world but their popularity is increasing.

## Varieties

| | BLOOM DETAILS | | GARDEN RECORD | |
|---|---|---|---|---|
| | Availability | Colour<br>Fragrance | Grown in garden/home | Performance during the year |
| **ANGELA RIPPON**<br>Popular for bedding and exhibiting. Grows 12–15 in. high — the blooms are quite large and growth is bushy. The flowers have 40 petals or more. Good disease resistance | ★★★ | Coral pink<br>-<br>Fragrant | | |
| **APRICOT SUNBLAZE**<br>One of the newer Miniatures, introduced in 1982. A new colour for the group — bright orange red. The flowers are small, cupped, full and fragrant. Height 12–15 in. | ★★ | Orange red<br>-<br>Fragrant | | |
| **BABY GOLD STAR**<br>Large blooms are the star feature — petals are few (12–15) and fragrance is slight. Colour fades to cream and fungicide spraying may be necessary. Height 12–15 in. | ★★ | Yellow<br>-<br>Slightly fragrant | | |
| **BABY MASQUERADE**<br>A Miniature version of the well-known Floribunda — flowers change from yellow to pink and finally to rosy red. Dead-head regularly. Grows 12–15 in. tall | ★★★★ | Yellow, changing to pink and red<br>-<br>No fragrance | | |
| **CINDERELLA**<br>A little beauty, 12 in. high. Small flowers, crowded with petals, on upright, thornless stems. These blooms are borne in clusters and last well in water. Foliage is abundant | ★★ | White, tinged pink<br>-<br>Slightly fragrant | | |
| **COLIBRI 79**<br>A compact, bushy variety which grows about 10 in. tall. The medium-sized blooms are fully double and are borne freely. Do not confuse with *Colibri*, introduced in 1959 | ★★★ | Orange, tinged pink<br>-<br>Slightly fragrant | | |
| **CORALIN**<br>The blooms are large and full — the colour may be pink, coral or light red. The 12–15 in. high stems are upright and densely clothed with bronzy leaves | ★★ | Orange red<br>-<br>No fragrance | | |
| **DARLING FLAME**<br>A recommended Miniature, despite lack of fragrance and decline in disease resistance. The red and yellow blooms are the attraction — they are borne profusely on 12 in. bushes | ★★ | Vermilion; golden yellow reverse<br>-<br>No fragrance | | |
| **DRESDEN DOLL**<br>A Miniature Moss Rose, growing about 10 in. high. The medium-sized blooms are semi-double — they have a classical H.T form and they appear freely | ★★★ | Pale pink<br>-<br>Fragrant | | |
| **EASTER MORNING**<br>Large blooms set amongst small, shiny leaves. These flowers bear 60 petals or more, yet rain resistance is good. Upright, 12–15 in. high and excellent for edging | ★★★ | Ivory<br>-<br>Slightly fragrant | | |
| **FIRE PRINCESS**<br>One of the many Miniatures bred by the American, Ralph Moore. Tall (18 in. high) with glossy, dark green foliage. The flowers darken with age — a good choice for bedding | ★★★ | Orange red<br>-<br>Slightly fragrant | | |
| **GREEN DIAMOND**<br>A talking point, certainly, but rather dull for garden display. The pink buds open into green rosettes on 12 in. bushes — these flowers are small and double. Popular with exhibitors | ★★ | Lime green<br>-<br>Slightly fragrant | | |
| **HULA GIRL**<br>An 18 in. bushy plant with flowers which are unusually large. These blooms are held stiffly erect — vivid and very full. Good indoors and out — an excellent specimen Miniature | ★★ | Salmon orange<br>-<br>Slightly fragrant | | |
| **LITTLE BUCKAROO**<br>Rather tall (15–18 in.) and spreading — good for the front of the border. The flowers are quite small with about 25 petals. Foliage is shiny and bronze-tinted | ★★★ | Bright red; white eye<br>-<br>Slightly fragrant | | |
| **LITTLE FLIRT**<br>A bi-colour with upright 15 in. stems and abundant foliage. The pointed buds open into bright flowers, but the colours fade with age. These blooms are small and full | ★★★ | Orange red; yellow reverse<br>-<br>Slightly fragrant | | |
| **MAGIC CARROUSEL**<br>An eye-catching variety for bedding, growing indoors or exhibiting. The unusual flowers are fairly large and double, appearing freely on the 15 in. bush | ★★★ | White, edged pink<br>-<br>Slightly fragrant | | |
| **MR BLUEBIRD**<br>Rather more blue than the equally popular *Lavender Jewel*, but it is often disappointing. Flowers may be few, stems may be spindly and the colour can appear insipid | ★★★ | Lavender<br>-<br>Slightly fragrant | | |

| | BLOOM DETAILS | | GARDEN RECORD | |
|---|---|---|---|---|
| | Availability | Colour — Fragrance | Grown in garden/ home | Performance during the year |
| **NEW PENNY**<br>One of the older Miniatures, introduced in 1962. The well-branched bush is densely clothed with dark glossy leaves. Recommended as a pot plant and for bedding. Height 12 in. | ★★ | Coppery pink — No fragrance | | |
| **ORANGE SUNBLAZE**<br>The start of Meilland's 'Sunblaze' collection in the 1980s. The blooms are large and last well in water. A popular choice these days for beds and patios. Grows 15 in. tall | ★★★ | Orange red — Slightly fragrant | | |
| **POUR TOI**<br>A favourite Miniature, highly rated for the beauty of its flowers and the attractive nature of the bush. Useful for edging — it flowers profusely and reaches about 9 in. | ★★★ | Creamy white — Slightly fragrant | | |
| **RED ACE**<br>A new flower form for Miniatures — dark red and velvety. Blooms are medium-sized and semi-double. Good for cutting and showing — bush height is 12 in. | ★★ | Dark crimson — Slightly fragrant | | |
| **RISE 'N' SHINE**<br>Perhaps the best of all yellow Miniatures. Long buds open into large blooms with a classic H.T. shape. Height is 15 in. You will have to spray against mildew | ★★ | Yellow — No fragrance | | |
| **ROSINA**<br>Often listed as *Josephine Wheatcroft*. An old favourite — flowers are moderately full, nicely shaped and bright yellow. It grows to about 12 in. and needs protection against disease | ★★★ | Yellow — Slightly fragrant | | |
| **SCARLET GEM**<br>The brightest of the red Miniatures. It is popular for growing indoors — the flowers appear freely and do not fade in the sun. Grows 15 in. tall. Prone to mildew | ★★ | Scarlet — Slightly fragrant | | |
| **SHERI ANNE**<br>A sweet-smelling variety for bedding, cutting and exhibiting. Growth is upright, reaching 15–18 in. Leaves are dark green and the flowers are large and bright | ★★ | Orange red — Fragrant | | |
| **STARINA**<br>A star of the Miniature world — the 18 in. bush bears very large vermilion flowers from early summer to November. Good for growing as a pot plant or for bedding | ★★★ | Orange red — Slightly fragrant | | |
| **STARS 'N' STRIPES**<br>A true novelty — the extra large blooms bear distinct white and cherry red stripes. The lax growth reaches about 15 in. Plant in groups for maximum effect | ★★ | White, striped red — No fragrance | | |
| **YELLOW DOLL**<br>Popular on the show bench and as a pot plant. The buds are borne singly or in clusters — each large flower has 50 or more petals. Height 15 in. | ★★★ | Pale yellow — Slightly fragrant | | |
| **YELLOW SUNBLAZE**<br>An addition by Meilland in 1983 to his 'Sunblaze' Miniatures. Small yellow blooms this time, occasionally edged with pink. They are double but the scent is not strong. Height 15 in. | ★★ | Bright yellow — Slightly fragrant | | |
| | | | | |
| | | | | |
| | | | | |

VARIETIES

**Fire Princess**

**Little Buckaroo**

**Magic Carrousel**

# CLIMBERS & RAMBLERS

## Varieties

| | Year of introduction | Type | Height Flowering period | Availability | Size of blooms Number of petals | Colour Fragrance |
|---|---|---|---|---|---|---|
| | **PLANT DETAILS** | | | | **BLOOM DETAILS** | |
| **ALBERIC BARBIER** A fine old pillar rose — especially useful where light and growing conditions are poor. The blooms are borne in clusters and the dark leaves are semi-evergreen | 1900 | Rambler | 20 ft — Midsummer | ★★★ | Medium — 45 petals | Cream — Fragrant |
| **ALBERTINE** Coppery buds open into scented blooms — pink with a touch of salmon. A favourite for many years — vigorous growth for covering walls and old trees. Spray against mildew | 1921 | Rambler | 15 ft — Early summer | ★★★★ | Medium — 25 petals | Pale pink — Very fragrant |
| **ALOHA** Another pink, this time with less vigour but more attractive flowers. It is recommended where slow and restricted growth are required. Foliage is healthy and attractive | 1949 | Large-flowered Climber | 9 ft — Repeat flowering | ★★★ | Large — 40 petals | Rose pink — Fragrant |
| **ALTISSIMO** The bold blooms bear a boss of golden stamens — the flowers appear in limited numbers throughout the summer. A healthy plant, quite widely used for covering walls and fences | 1967 | Large-flowered Climber | 10 ft — Repeat flowering | ★★★ | Medium — 7 petals | Blood red — Slightly fragrant |
| **AMERICAN PILLAR** The appeal of this old and popular variety lies in the profusion of extra-large trusses which appear in July. A troublesome rose — fungicide spraying and drastic pruning are needed | 1902 | Rambler | 20 ft — Midsummer | ★★★★ | Small — 7 petals | Deep pink; white eye — No fragrance |
| **BANTRY BAY** The flat blooms appear fairly regularly — the trusses bear many flowers and this variety is recommended for cutting. A restrained Climber for fences and walls | 1967 | Large-flowered Climber | 9 ft — Repeat flowering | ★★ | Large — 15 petals | Rose pink — Slightly fragrant |
| **BREATH OF LIFE** The blooms are borne singly or in small clusters — the shape is classic H.T and the scent is quite strong and unusual. An excellent cutting rose, according to the catalogues | 1982 | Large-flowered Climber | 9 ft — Repeat flowering | ★★★★ | Large — 30 petals | Apricot — Fragrant |
| **CASINO** This variety has many good points — scent, classic-shaped blooms, healthy leaves, prolonged flowering season, etc. But it is too delicate for cold and exposed sites | 1963 | Large-flowered Climber | 10 ft — Repeat flowering | ★★★★ | Large — 30 petals | Primrose yellow — Fragrant |
| **CECILE BRUNNER, CLIMBING** The climbing sport of *Cécile Brunner*, a dainty Shrub Rose. Not particularly free-flowering, and blooming is only sporadic once the June flush is over | 1894 | Climbing China Rose | 20 ft — Repeat flowering | ★★★ | Small — 25 petals | Shell pink — Slightly fragrant |
| **COMPASSION** It is no surprise that this rose has become so popular. The H.T-type blooms are large, attractively coloured and sweetly scented. The stems are vigorous and the leaves are healthy | 1973 | Large-flowered Climber | 9 ft — Repeat flowering | ★★★★★ | Large — 40 petals | Pink, shaded apricot — Very fragrant |
| **CRIMSON GLORY, CLIMBING** There is no escaping the faults — disease-ridden in summer and blooms that purple with age. But the virtues are impressive — velvety flowers with an outstanding scent | 1946 | Climbing Hybrid Tea | 10 ft — Repeat flowering | ★★ | Medium — 30 petals | Deep crimson — Very fragrant |
| **CRIMSON SHOWER** A vigorous Rambler with small rosette-shaped flowers. The flowering season lasts throughout August. It is not prone to mildew — surprising for a Rambler. Good for trellises | 1951 | Rambler | 12 ft — Late summer | ★★★ | Small — 20 petals | Crimson — Slightly fragrant |
| **DANSE DU FEU** Well known for the brightness of its blooms and its free-flowering habit. A good choice for a wall or pergola — it flowers during its first season | 1954 | Large-flowered Climber | 8 ft — Repeat flowering | ★★★★ | Medium — 35 petals | Orange scarlet — No fragrance |
| **DOROTHY PERKINS** Introduced in the year Queen Victoria died, old *Dorothy* is still grown in many gardens. A mass of pink flowers appears in August, but it is not a good choice nowadays | 1901 | Rambler | 15 ft — Late summer | ★★★ | Small — 35 petals | Rose pink — Slightly fragrant |
| **DORTMUND** Healthy and very hardy, as you would expect from a Kordes-bred Climber. Both flowers and trusses are large and eye-catching — recommended for pergolas and fences | 1955 | Kordesii Climber | 8 ft — Repeat flowering | ★★ | Large — 5 petals | Red; white eye — No fragrance |
| **DUBLIN BAY** No red Climber blooms more freely, according to some of the experts. The flowers are nicely shaped and the foliage is abundant. Unfortunately, it occasionally forgets to climb | 1976 | Large-flowered Climber | 8 ft — Repeat flowering | ★★ | Large — 25 petals | Deep red — Slightly fragrant |
| **EMILY GRAY** An old favourite with flowers the colour of chamois leather and leaves which are almost evergreen. Attractive, but not particularly free-flowering. Prune very lightly | 1918 | Rambler | 15 ft — Midsummer | ★★★★ | Small — 25 petals | Buff yellow — Fragrant |
| **ENA HARKNESS, CLIMBING** The drooping blooms are a drawback on the bush but are an advantage on the climbing form. There is beauty of colour, form and fragrance. Late season blooming is disappointing | 1954 | Climbing Hybrid Tea | 12 ft — Repeat flowering | ★★★ | Large — 30 petals | Crimson scarlet — Very fragrant |

A class of roses which if tied to a support can be made to climb. There are two basic groups Ramblers have long, pliable stems and generally bear large trusses of small flowers. Growth is vigorous and there is nearly always a single flush of flowers in summer. They have lost much of their popularity as regular fungicide spraying is necessary and cutting out old wood each year is a tiresome chore. Climbers have stiffer stems and the flowers are usually larger and the trusses smaller. The framework of wood is more or less permanent, so pruning and maintenance are easier.

**VARIETIES**

| rown in arden | Year of planting (if known) | Supplier | Performance during the year | Problems during the year | Included in Rose Analysis |
|---|---|---|---|---|---|
| | | | | | C & R |
| | | | | | C & R |
| | | | | | C & R |
| | | | | | No |
| | | | | | No |
| | | | | | No |
| | | | | | C & R |
| | | | | | No |
| | | | | | No |
| | | | | | C & R |
| | | | | | No |
| | | | | | No |
| | | | | | C & R |
| | | | | | No |
| | | | | | No |
| | | | | | No |
| | | | | | C & R |
| | | | | | No |

**GARDEN RECORD**

# CLIMBERS & RAMBLERS

## Varieties

| | Year of introduction | Type | Height / Flowering period | Availability | Size of blooms / Number of petals | Colour / Fragrance |
|---|---|---|---|---|---|---|
| **ETOILE DE HOLLANDE, CLIMBING** <br> The climbing sport of this once popular H.T is superior to its parent. An excellent choice for clothing a wall — the summer display is impressive but the autumn show may disappoint | 1931 | Climbing Hybrid Tea | 12 ft <br> Repeat flowering | ★★★ | Large <br> 40 petals | Deep red <br> Very fragrant |
| **EXCELSA** <br> Sometimes called *Red Dorothy Perkins*, this old rampant grower is still a popular variety. Festooned with globular flowers, it is useful for arches and pergolas | 1909 | Rambler | 15 ft <br> Midsummer | ★★★ | Small <br> 35 petals | Crimson; white centre <br> No fragrance |
| **FRANCOIS JURANVILLE** <br> Here is everyone's idea of an old-fashioned rose — large open blooms with a heady scent. The stems are long and flexible with few thorns. Good for a large screen | 1906 | Rambler | 20 ft <br> Early summer | ★★★ | Large <br> 25 petals | Pale pink <br> Fragrant |
| **GALWAY BAY** <br> Blooms are well-formed and borne in profusion — they appear in clusters. Growth is restrained — this one is for a pillar or arch and not for screening a wall | 1966 | Large-flowered Climber | 8 ft <br> Repeat flowering | ★★ | Large <br> 25 petals | Pink <br> Slightly fragrant |
| **GLOIRE DE DIJON** <br> Like *Excelsa*, this oldie keeps its place in the catalogues. Still a good choice for walls, but you will have to spray against mildew. It flowers early and continually | 1853 | Noisette Climber | 12 ft <br> Repeat flowering | ★★★ | Large <br> 50 petals | Buff yellow <br> Fragrant |
| **GOLDEN SHOWERS** <br> The No.1 choice amongst yellow Climbers. Its growth is restrained and the flowers are rather loose. But it is a winner — prolonged flowering, excellent health and bright blooms | 1956 | Large-flowered Climber | 8 ft <br> Repeat flowering | ★★★★★ | Large <br> 25 petals | Golden yellow <br> Fragrant |
| **GUINEE** <br> A distinctive variety because of its flower colour — dark red in sunlight, almost black on dull days. A mass of blooms in June — disappointing later. The stems are stiff and rigid | 1938 | Large-flowered Climber | 15 ft <br> Repeat flowering | ★★★ | Large <br> 35 petals | Very dark red <br> Very fragrant |
| **HANDEL** <br> You can't miss this one — the strawberry-tipped petals are unlike other Climbers. The flowers are borne in clusters and the stems bear few thorns. Spray against mildew | 1965 | Large-flowered Climber | 10 ft <br> Repeat flowering | ★★★★★ | Medium <br> 20 petals | Cream, edged rosy pink <br> Slightly fragrant |
| **HIGHFIELD** <br> A sport of *Compassion*, it has never rivalled the popularity of its parent. Most of *Compassion*'s properties are there, but both bloom size and scent are somewhat reduced | 1981 | Large-flowered Climber | 9 ft <br> Repeat flowering | ★★ | Medium <br> 40 petals | Pale yellow <br> Fragrant |
| **ICEBERG, CLIMBING** <br> Surely the climbing sport of the Queen of the Whites should have been a winner. There is nothing wrong with the variety, but it never became a top-selling Climber | 1968 | Climbing Floribunda | 10 ft <br> Repeat flowering | ★★★★ | Medium <br> 25 petals | White <br> Slightly fragrant |
| **LADY SYLVIA, CLIMBING** <br> A rampant grower which will reach 20 ft or more, even under conditions which leave much to be desired. Occasionally more than one flush appears. Do not prune heavily | 1933 | Climbing Hybrid Tea | 20 ft <br> Late summer | ★★ | Medium <br> 30 petals | Pale pink; yellow at base <br> Very fragrant |
| **LEVERKUSEN** <br> Another one from the Kordes stable — healthy, hardy and free-flowering. Large clusters of flowers appear in June, and these are followed by flushes later in the season | 1954 | Kordesii Climber | 9 ft <br> Repeat flowering | ★★★ | Medium <br> 20 petals | Pale yellow <br> Slightly fragrant |
| **MADAME ALFRED CARRIERE** <br> There must be a reason why a 100 year old rose survives in the catalogues. This one grows happily on a north-facing wall — not many modern ones can do that | 1879 | Noisette Climber | 20 ft <br> Repeat flowering | ★★★ | Large <br> 35 petals | White, flushed pink <br> Very fragrant |
| **MADAME GREGOIRE STAECHELIN** <br> A frilly-petalled old favourite. In June the plant is almost covered by the blooms, but in a few weeks they are gone. Large hips follow | 1927 | Large-flowered Climber | 20 ft <br> Early summer | ★★★ | Large <br> 20 petals | Pink, shaded crimson <br> Very fragrant |
| **MAIGOLD** <br> The reason why *Maigold* is in all the best-seller lists is easy to see — the large, sweetly-scented blooms appear in May. These flowers are cupped and the stems are thorny | 1953 | Large-flowered Climber | 10 ft <br> Early summer | ★★★★ | Large <br> 15 petals | Bronze yellow <br> Fragrant |
| **MASQUERADE, CLIMBING** <br> Like the bush *Masquerade*, the flowers change colour as they mature. To prolong the display you must dead-head regularly. Recommended for pillars and fences | 1958 | Climbing Floribunda | 8 ft <br> Repeat flowering | ★★★ | Medium <br> 15 petals | Yellow, then pink and red <br> Slightly fragrant |
| **MERMAID** <br> Introduced generations ago, and still popular — the clusters of bold flowers are the reason. Its constitution is not good — temperamental, frost-sensitive and slow to establish | 1918 | Large-flowered Climber | 25 ft <br> Repeat flowering | ★★★ | Large <br> 5 petals | Primrose amber <br> Fragrant |
| **MORNING JEWEL** <br> A hardy variety which is quite happy on an east wall. It blooms all summer long against a backcloth of shiny leaves. Useful for clothing fences | 1969 | Large-flowered Climber | 8 ft <br> Repeat flowering | ★★ | Large <br> 20 petals | Pink <br> Slightly fragrant |
| **NEW DAWN** <br> The star amongst the Ramblers. The growth is restrained for this group, and flowers appear throughout the summer. The blooms are not large, but they do appear in large clusters | 1930 | Rambler | 12 ft <br> Repeat flowering | ★★★★★ | Small <br> 25 petals | Shell pink <br> Fragrant |
| **PARKDIREKTOR RIGGERS** <br> Not many petals, but the trusses are huge. Dead-head regularly. Free-flowering and hardy — suitable for a north wall. Unlike other Kordesii types, it is susceptible to mildew | 1957 | Kordesii Climber | 12 ft <br> Repeat flowering | ★★★ | Medium <br> 15 petals | Blood red <br> Slightly fragrant |
| **PAUL'S SCARLET CLIMBER** <br> The top climbing red for many years — now well past its prime. The cupped blooms appear for about a month and are then gone. Prone to mildew | 1916 | Rambler | 10 ft <br> Early summer | ★★★★ | Small <br> 25 petals | Scarlet, shaded crimson <br> Slightly fragrant |

| Grown in garden | Year of planting (if known) | Supplier | Performance during the year | Problems during the year | Included in Rose Analysis |
|---|---|---|---|---|---|
| | | | | | C & R |
| | | | | | No |
| | | | | | No |
| | | | | | No |
| | | | | | C & R |
| | | | | | C & R |
| | | | | | No |
| | | | | | C & R |
| | | | | | No |
| | | | | | C & R |
| | | | | | No |
| | | | | | No |
| | | | | | No |
| | | | | | No |
| | | | | | C & R |
| | | | | | No |
| | | | | | C & R |
| | | | | | C & R |
| | | | | | C & R |
| | | | | | No |
| | | | | | C & R |

**GARDEN RECORD**

VARIETIES

# CLIMBERS & RAMBLERS

## Varieties

| | Year of introduction | Type | Height — Flowering period | Availability | Size of blooms — Number of petals | Colour — Fragrance |
|---|---|---|---|---|---|---|
| | | PLANT DETAILS | | | BLOOM DETAILS | |
| **PINK PERPETUE**<br>Popular and free-flowering. Hardy, too — it can be grown on a north wall. The blooms appear in clusters — a 'Cluster-flowered Climber' according to the new classification | 1965 | Large-flowered Climber | 8 ft — Repeat flowering | ★★★★★ | Medium — 30 petals | Rose pink; carmine reverse — Slightly fragrant |
| **ROSA FILIPES KIFTSGATE**<br>Like *Mermaid*, a giant Rambler in the top 10 list of climbing roses. Use it to cover sheds or old trees — don't flatten it against the house | 1954 | Rambler | 25 ft — Midsummer | ★★★★ | Small — 5 petals | Creamy white — Fragrant |
| **ROSY MANTLE**<br>A wiry-stemmed Climber which has *New Dawn* as one of its parents. The blooms are like an H.T — the scent is strong and the flowering season is a long one | 1968 | Large-flowered Climber | 9 ft — Repeat flowering | ★★ | Large — 25 petals | Rose pink — Fragrant |
| **ROYAL GOLD**<br>The catalogue description has made this a popular variety — large H.T-type blooms in brilliant yellow. Unfortunately it does not flower freely and is damaged by frost | 1957 | Large-flowered Climber | 8 ft — Repeat flowering | ★★★ | Large — 35 petals | Deep yellow — Slightly fragrant |
| **SANDERS WHITE RAMBLER**<br>Old, but both popularity and health remain. Excellent for clothing arches and fences. Trusses are large and perfumed — leaves are bright green and glossy | 1912 | Rambler | 10 ft — Midsummer | ★★★ | Small — 40 petals | White — Fragrant |
| **SCHOOLGIRL**<br>Good for cutting and for covering a wall. The colour is unusual — the shape of the bloom is classic H.T. Prolonged but not profuse flowering. Main problem is the loss of lower leaves | 1964 | Large-flowered Climber | 10 ft — Repeat flowering | ★★★★★ | Large — 25 petals | Apricot orange — Fragrant |
| **SEAGULL**<br>Large trusses of single flowers which bear a prominent disc of golden stamens. Widely used for scrambling up and covering old trees. Growth is very vigorous | 1907 | Rambler | 20 ft — Midsummer | ★★★ | Small — 7 petals | White — Fragrant |
| **SWAN LAKE**<br>A Climber to choose if you want a white rose with the form of an H.T. Free-flowering and not spoilt by rain, but highly susceptible to mildew and black spot | 1968 | Large-flowered Climber | 8 ft — Repeat flowering | ★★★ | Large — 50 petals | White, tinged pink — Slightly fragrant |
| **VEILCHENBLAU**<br>The masses of blooms in summer are unusual — perhaps closer to blue than any other rose. Mature blooms, however, are slate grey. The stems have very few thorns | 1909 | Rambler | 15 ft — Midsummer | ★★★ | Small — 15 petals | Violet, fading to grey — Fragrant |
| **WEDDING DAY**<br>A rampant Rambler like *Rosa Filipes Kiftsgate*. Flower trusses appear in July and August — cream fading to pinky white. Very vigorous, but is not keen on exposed sites | 1950 | Rambler | 25 ft — Midsummer | ★★★ | Small — 5 petals | Creamy white — Fragrant |
| **WHITE COCKADE**<br>A rival to *Swan Lake* as the best white with H.T form. The flowers last well in water. Vigorous, healthy and free-flowering. Grow it as a full bush or to clothe a fence | 1969 | Large-flowered Climber | 7 ft — Repeat flowering | ★★★ | Medium — 25 petals | White — Slightly fragrant |
| **ZEPHIRINE DROUHIN**<br>This almost thornless rose can be grown as a shrub, hedge, pillar, ground cover or as a climbing plant against a wall. Dead-head regularly and spray with a fungicide | 1868 | Climbing Bourbon Rose | 10 ft — Repeat flowering | ★★★★★ | Medium — 20 petals | Carmine pink — Very fragrant |
| | | | | | | |
| | | | | | | |

**Albertine**

**Breath of Life**

**Compassion**

# GARDEN RECORD

| Grown in garden | Year of planting (if known) | Supplier | Performance during the year | Problems during the year | Included in Rose Analysis |
|---|---|---|---|---|---|
| | | | | | C & R |
| | | | | | C & R |
| | | | | | C & R |
| | | | | | No |
| | | | | | No |
| | | | | | C & R |
| | | | | | No |
| | | | | | C & R |
| | | | | | No |
| | | | | | No |
| | | | | | No |
| | | | | | C & R OGR SC |
| | | | | | |
| | | | | | |

VARIETIES

*Handel*

*Pink Perpêtue*

*Schoolgirl*

# SHRUB ROSES

## Varieties

| | PLANT DETAILS | | | | BLOOM DETAILS | |
|---|---|---|---|---|---|---|
| | Year of introduction<br>Growth type | Height (H)<br>x<br>Width (W) | Type<br>Flowering period | Availability | Size of blooms<br>Number of petals | Colour<br>Fragrance |
| **ANGELINA**<br>A compact bush — vigorous, healthy and suitable for the small garden. A number of good points which should have made it popular ... but didn't | 1975<br>—<br>Bushy | 3½ ft (H)<br>x<br>3½ ft (W) | Modern Shrub Rose<br>—<br>Repeat flowering | ★★ | Large<br>—<br>15 petals | Deep pink; white eye<br>—<br>Slightly fragra |
| **AUSTRIAN COPPER**<br>Also known as the *Capucine Rose*. Steeped in history, but not one for the average garden. Flowering period lasts for about 2 weeks and the leaves are prone to mildew | pre 1590<br>—<br>Arching | 5 ft (H)<br>x<br>4 ft (W) | Species Rose<br>—<br>Midsummer | ★★ | Small<br>—<br>5 petals | Dark orange, yellow revers<br>—<br>No fragrance |
| **BALLERINA**<br>A popular Shrub — the tiny flowers form hydrangea-like heads. The pale green leaves are healthy and this is one to grow as a hedge or in the shrub border | 1937<br>—<br>Bushy | 3½ ft (H)<br>x<br>3 ft (W) | Modern Shrub Rose<br>—<br>Repeat flowering | ★★★★ | Small<br>—<br>5 petals | Pale pink; white eye<br>—<br>Slightly fragra |
| **BLANC DOUBLE DE COUBERT**<br>Still a favourite after 100 years. The large, sweet-smelling flowers appear from June onwards. Healthy, but leaves are sparse and the bush has a bare appearance | 1892<br>—<br>Bushy | 5½ ft (H)<br>x<br>5 ft (W) | Rugosa Shrub<br>—<br>Repeat flowering | ★★★★ | Large<br>—<br>10 petals | White<br>—<br>Very fragrant |
| **BLANCHE MOREAU**<br>One of the best Moss Roses — buds are covered with brownish 'moss'. Flowers are full with a central green button. Flower trusses appear in June | 1880<br>—<br>Open | 6 ft (H)<br>x<br>7 ft (W) | Moss Rose<br>—<br>Midsummer | ★★ | Large<br>—<br>35 petals | White<br>—<br>Fragrant |
| **BONICA 82**<br>A large ground-cover Shrub, covering the soil with its lower branches. Make sure you pick the right variety — the old *Bonica* is a red-flowered bush. This one is *Bonica 82* | 1984<br>—<br>Procumbent | 5 ft (H)<br>x<br>3 ft (W) | Modern Shrub Rose<br>—<br>Repeat flowering | ★★★ | Medium<br>—<br>25 petals | Pink<br>—<br>Slightly fragrant |
| **BOULE DE NEIGE**<br>Snowball in English — a good name for this rose with its white, ball-like blooms borne in small clusters. There are problems — black spot and rain damage to the blooms | 1867<br>—<br>Upright | 5 ft (H)<br>x<br>3 ft (W) | Bourbon Rose<br>—<br>Repeat flowering | ★★★ | Large<br>—<br>50 petals | Ivory<br>—<br>Very fragrant |
| **BUFF BEAUTY**<br>A popular Shrub for hedging, cutting and planting in the border. The foliage is purple tinted — attractive, but also prone to mildew. Flowers fade to ivory with age | 1939<br>—<br>Arching | 4 ft (H)<br>x<br>4 ft (W) | Hybrid Musk<br>—<br>Repeat flowering | ★★★★ | Large<br>—<br>50 petals | Pale apricot<br>—<br>Fragrant |
| **CANARY BIRD**<br>Very few Shrub Roses outsell *Canary Bird*. The reason is simple — it heralds in the rose flowering season in May. Blooms appear along the ferny-leaved stems | 1907<br>—<br>Arching | 6 ft (H)<br>x<br>6 ft (W) | Species Rose<br>—<br>Late spring | ★★★★★ | Small<br>—<br>5 petals | Canary yellow<br>—<br>Fragrant |
| **CANDY ROSE**<br>A wide-spreading ground cover. There are several good points for this addition to this type of rose — it is repeat flowering and will also grow in quite shady conditions | 1982<br>—<br>Procumbent | 3 ft (H)<br>x<br>6 ft (W) | Modern Shrub Rose<br>—<br>Repeat flowering | ★★ | Medium<br>—<br>15 petals | Pink<br>—<br>No fragrance |
| **CECILE BRUNNER**<br>This is the *Sweetheart Rose*. Grow it if you love Victorian roses or if you want flowers for your buttonhole. Not good for garden display — the foliage is sparse | 1881<br>—<br>Open | 2½ ft (H)<br>x<br>2½ ft (W) | China Rose<br>—<br>Repeat flowering | ★★★ | Small<br>—<br>25 petals | Shell pink<br>—<br>Slightly fragrant |
| **CELESTIAL**<br>A typical Alba — vigorous, hardy and trouble-free. The leaves are grey-green — a useful variety for hedging. Free-flowering — the blooms soon open wide | 1780<br>—<br>Upright | 6 ft (H)<br>x<br>4 ft (W) | Alba Rose<br>—<br>Midsummer | ★★★ | Medium<br>—<br>25 petals | Blush pink<br>—<br>Fragrant |
| **CHAPEAU DE NAPOLEON**<br>The buds bear a distinctive winged extension — hence the common name 'Napoleon's Hat'. The flowers are globular with an old-fashioned scent | 1827<br>—<br>Open | 5 ft (H)<br>x<br>4 ft (W) | Centifolia Rose<br>—<br>Midsummer | ★★★ | Large<br>—<br>30 petals | Rose pink<br>—<br>Fragrant |
| **CHINATOWN**<br>Perhaps the top-selling Shrub Rose — popular for hedging, back of the border or as a specimen bush. Rain-resistant, healthy and tolerant of poor conditions | 1963<br>—<br>Bushy | 5 ft (H)<br>x<br>4 ft (W) | Modern Shrub Rose<br>—<br>Repeat flowering | ★★★★★ | Large<br>—<br>25 petals | Yellow, edged pink<br>—<br>Fragrant |
| **COMMON MOSS ROSE**<br>The best of the Moss Roses — stems and buds bear green 'moss'. The June/July blooms are globular at first, opening flat when mature. Spray against mildew | 1700<br>—<br>Open | 4 ft (H)<br>x<br>4 ft (W) | Moss Rose<br>—<br>Midsummer | ★★★ | Large<br>—<br>35 petals | Rose pink<br>—<br>Fragrant |
| **COMPLICATA**<br>Nobody knows where or when this variety was born, but it remains in the catalogues. Its outstanding feature is the size of the flowers — 4–5 in. across | ?<br>—<br>Arching | 6 ft (H)<br>x<br>8 ft (W) | Gallica Rose<br>—<br>Midsummer | ★★★ | Large<br>—<br>5 petals | Pink; white eye<br>—<br>Slightly fragra |
| **CORNELIA**<br>The large trusses and free-flowering habit make this variety a popular Shrub Rose. The leaves are unusually dark and the flowers are rosette-like. Good for hedging | 1925<br>—<br>Spreading | 5 ft (H)<br>x<br>7 ft (W) | Hybrid Musk<br>—<br>Repeat flowering | ★★★ | Small<br>—<br>20 petals | Apricot pink<br>—<br>Very fragrant |
| **DOROTHY WHEATCROFT**<br>The trusses are borne on long stems — the weight of flowers causes them to bow their heads if not supported. The bush looks lanky — put it at the back of the border | 1960<br>—<br>Upright | 4½ ft (H)<br>x<br>3 ft (W) | Modern Shrub Rose<br>—<br>Repeat flowering | ★★ | Large<br>—<br>15 petals | Orange red, flushed scarle<br>—<br>Slightly fragra |

A large class of bush roses with only one feature in common — they are not Floribundas, Hybrid Teas or Miniatures. The typical Shrub is taller than a bedding rose, but heights vary from a ground-hugging 18 in. to a towering 10 ft. Some flower once only, but there are many which are repeat flowering. In addition there is every flower form, ranging from tiny 5-petalled types to large shapely blooms which would be at home in the Hybrid Tea section. Nearly all the types listed here have been around for many years, but a few are recent introductions.

| GARDEN RECORD | | | | | Included in Rose Analysis |
|---|---|---|---|---|---|
| Grown in garden | Year of planting (if known) | Supplier | Performance during the year | Problems during the year | |
| | | | | | No |
| | | | | | No |
| | | | | | SH |
| | | | | | OGR SH |
| | | | | | No |
| | | | | | No |
| | | | | | No |
| | | | | | SH |
| | | | | | SH |
| | | | | | No |
| | | | | | OGR |
| | | | | | OGR |
| | | | | | No |
| | | | | | BCF SH |
| | | | | | No |
| | | | | | No |
| | | | | | No |
| | | | | | No |

VARIETIES

# SHRUB ROSES

## Varieties

| | PLANT DETAILS | | | | BLOOM DETAILS | |
|---|---|---|---|---|---|---|
| | Year of introduction Growth type | Height (H) x Width (W) | Type Flowering period | Availability | Size of blooms Number of petals | Colour Fragrance |
| **FELICIA**<br>A Shrub Rose noted for the length of its flowering season — from June to November. Young flowers are shapely and the musk-like scent is strong. Good for hedging | 1928<br>—<br>Spreading | 5 ft (H)<br>x<br>7 ft (W) | Hybrid Musk<br>—<br>Repeat flowering | ★★★ | Medium<br>—<br>20 petals | Apricot pink<br>—<br>Very fragrant |
| **FIONA**<br>A ground-cover rose, spreading its stems over a large area. Both trusses and leaves are quite small, but the overall effect is very colourful | 1983<br>—<br>Procumbent | 3½ ft (H)<br>x<br>6 ft (W) | Modern Shrub Rose<br>—<br>Repeat flowering | ★★★ | Small<br>—<br>25 petals | Blood red<br>—<br>Slightly fragrant |
| **F J GROOTENDORST**<br>Tough, like other Rugosas, so you can depend upon it under poor conditions. The flowers are small and frilly-edged, giving a carnation-like effect | 1918<br>—<br>Open | 5 ft (H)<br>x<br>5 ft (W) | Rugosa Shrub<br>—<br>Repeat flowering | ★★★ | Small<br>—<br>25 petals | Crimson<br>—<br>No fragrance |
| **FOUNTAIN**<br>In 1971 the supreme RNRS award went to a Shrub Rose — a most unusual occurrence! The velvety red flowers appealed to the judges. Popular appeal was less | 1972<br>—<br>Upright | 5 ft (H)<br>x<br>3 ft (W) | Modern Shrub Rose<br>—<br>Repeat flowering | ★★★ | Large<br>—<br>35 petals | Blood red<br>—<br>Fragrant |
| **FRAU DAGMAR HARTOPP**<br>Popular, like several other Rugosas. Small for the family, but one of the best. All the good properties are there — health, scent, continuous flowering, hardiness and hips | 1914<br>—<br>Bushy | 4½ ft (H)<br>x<br>3½ ft (W) | Rugosa Shrub<br>—<br>Repeat flowering | ★★★★ | Large<br>—<br>5 petals | Shell pink<br>—<br>Very fragrant |
| **FRAU KARL DRUSCHKI**<br>Pink buds open into pure white blooms set against rich green foliage. Follow the rules — prune lightly, spray against mildew and peg down long shoots | 1901<br>—<br>Upright | 5 ft (H)<br>x<br>4 ft (W) | Hybrid Perpetual<br>—<br>Repeat flowering | ★★ | Large<br>—<br>35 petals | White<br>—<br>No fragrance |
| **FRED LOADS**<br>Not many petals but each flower is large and colourful. The trusses are even more impressive, reaching 18 in. across. The bushes can look top-heavy | 1967<br>—<br>Upright | 6 ft (H)<br>x<br>4 ft (W) | Modern Shrub Rose<br>—<br>Repeat flowering | ★★★ | Large<br>—<br>8 petals | Orange vermilion<br>—<br>Fragrant |
| **FRUHLINGSGOLD**<br>The most popular of the 'Fruhlings' roses. Surprising, perhaps — it blooms for only about 2 weeks. But look at a mature bush in full flower and you will see why | 1937<br>—<br>Arching | 8 ft (H)<br>x<br>7 ft (W) | Species Rose<br>—<br>Early summer | ★★★★ | Large<br>—<br>10 petals | Creamy yellow<br>—<br>Fragrant |
| **FRUHLINGSMORGEN**<br>Another Kordes hybrid of the Scotch Briar, shorter and bushier than its yellow sister described above. The autumn flush is less prolific than the summer one | 1942<br>—<br>Open | 6 ft (H)<br>x<br>5 ft (W) | Species Rose<br>—<br>June and September | ★★★ | Medium<br>—<br>5 petals | Deep pink yellow centre<br>—<br>Fragrant |
| **GOLDEN WINGS**<br>A favourite amongst large-flowered yellow Shrub Roses. You can't do much better — there is disease- and rain-resistance plus scent, but you must dead-head regularly | 1956<br>—<br>Bushy | 6 ft (H)<br>x<br>5 ft (W) | Modern Shrub Rose<br>—<br>Repeat flowering | ★★★★ | Large<br>—<br>8 petals | Pale yellow<br>—<br>Fragrant |
| **GRAHAM THOMAS**<br>A new contender for the large yellow crown. The flower is paeony-like — a modern colour for an old-fashioned shape. The fragrance is tea-like. An excellent choice | 1983<br>—<br>Arching | 4 ft (H)<br>x<br>4 ft (W) | Modern Shrub Rose<br>—<br>Repeat flowering | ★★★ | Large<br>—<br>25 petals | Deep yellow<br>—<br>Fragrant |
| **GROUSE**<br>One of the 'game bird' ground-cover roses — others are *Partridge* (white) and *Pheasant* (rose pink). All produce wide-spreading, ground-hugging branches | 1984<br>—<br>Procumbent | 1½ ft (H)<br>x<br>8 ft (W) | Modern Shrub Rose<br>—<br>Repeat flowering | ★★ | Small<br>—<br>5 petals | Pale pink<br>—<br>Fragrant |
| **JOSEPH'S COAT**<br>Something different — a Shrub Rose which changes petal colour from yellow to red as the flower ages. Large and colourful, but it has never become popular | 1964<br>—<br>Open | 6 ft (H)<br>x<br>7 ft (W) | Modern Shrub Rose<br>—<br>Repeat flowering | ★★★ | Medium<br>—<br>25 petals | Yellow, changing to orange and red<br>—<br>Slightly fragrant |
| **LADY PENZANCE**<br>Another novelty — this hybrid of the Sweet Briar is grown for the apple-like fragrance of its leaves rather than for its flowers. The shrub is only in bloom for 1–2 weeks | 1894<br>—<br>Open | 6 ft (H)<br>x<br>6 ft (W) | Species Rose<br>—<br>Early summer | ★★★ | Small<br>—<br>5 petals | Copper, yellow centre<br>—<br>Very fragrant |

**Ballerina**

**Bonica 82**

**Canary Bird**

## GARDEN RECORD

| Grown in garden | Year of planting (if known) | Supplier | Performance during the year | Problems during the year | Included in Rose Analysis |
|---|---|---|---|---|---|
| | | | | | SH |
| | | | | | No |
| | | | | | No |
| | | | | | SH |
| | | | | | SH |
| | | | | | No |
| | | | | | E SH |
| | | | | | SH |
| | | | | | No |
| | | | | | SH |
| | | | | | N SH |
| | | | | | No |
| | | | | | No |
| | | | | | No |

VARIETIES

**Chinatown**

**Graham Thomas**

**Joseph's Coat**

# SHRUB ROSES

## Varieties

| | PLANT DETAILS | | | | BLOOM DETAILS | |
|---|---|---|---|---|---|---|
| | Year of introduction<br>Growth type | Height (H)<br>x<br>Width (W) | Type<br>Flowering period | Availability | Size of blooms<br>Number of petals | Colour<br>Fragrance |
| **LITTLE WHITE PET**<br>This little bush starts to flower in midsummer, producing pompon-like blooms in large clusters. These may be numerous enough to cover the plant completely | 1879<br>Spreading | 2½ ft (H)<br>x<br>2 ft (W) | Polyantha Rose<br>Repeat flowering | ★★★ | Small<br>35 petals | White<br>Fragrant |
| **MADAME HARDY**<br>Large flat blooms — white with a green eye. As with all Damask Roses the stems are lax, so some support is necessary. The blooms are damaged by rain | 1832<br>Open | 6 ft (H)<br>x<br>5 ft (W) | Damask Rose<br>Midsummer | ★★★ | Large<br>50 petals | White<br>Fragrant |
| **MADAME ISAAC PEREIRE**<br>A grand old-fashioned rose — tall, very strongly scented and with blooms which are extra large and often misshapen. The stems need to be supported | 1881<br>Open | 8 ft (H)<br>x<br>6 ft (W) | Bourbon Rose<br>Repeat flowering | ★★★ | Large<br>50 petals | Deep carmine pink<br>Very fragrant |
| **MARGUERITE HILLING**<br>A sport of Nevada, but nowhere near as widely grown. Similar to its parent apart from flower colour. It needs space and also early spraying to prevent black spot | 1959<br>Arching | 7 ft (H)<br>x<br>7 ft (W) | Modern Shrub Rose<br>June & September | ★★★ | Large<br>10 petals | Pink, shade deep pink<br>Slightly fragrant |
| **MARJORIE FAIR**<br>Similar to its parent Ballerina in growth habit and flower form, but the petals are red rather than pink. Colourful and healthy, but not very popular | 1978<br>Bushy | 3½ ft (H)<br>x<br>3 ft (W) | Modern Shrub Rose<br>Repeat flowering | ★★★ | Small<br>5 petals | Red; white centre<br>Slightly fragrant |
| **MARY ROSE**<br>Here is a variety to fool you. A typical Victorian rose — large, very full, cupped and full of fragrance. But it is in fact a rose of the 1980s | 1983<br>Bushy | 4 ft (H)<br>x<br>4 ft (W) | Modern Shrub Rose<br>Repeat flowering | ★★★ | Large<br>50 petals | Rose pink<br>Very fragrant |
| **MAX GRAF**<br>The first and still very popular low-growing ground cover rose. The stems trail over the soil to produce a dense mat. Useful for growing over a wall | 1919<br>Trailing | 1½ ft (H)<br>x<br>5 ft (W) | Rugosa Shrub<br>Midsummer | ★★★★ | Medium<br>5 petals | Pink; white centre<br>Fragrant |
| **NEVADA**<br>The first (and main) flush in June covers the whole bush with creamy flowers. After more than 60 years it is still one of Britain's favourite Shrub Roses | 1927<br>Arching | 7 ft (H)<br>x<br>7 ft (W) | Modern Shrub Rose<br>June & September | ★★★★ | Large<br>10 petals | Creamy white<br>Slightly fragrant |
| **NOZOMI**<br>An often-used ground cover, but it is not wide-spreading. Useful for edging, but it is not as colourful or weed suppressing as modern ground covers such as Grouse | 1968<br>Trailing | 1½ ft (H)<br>x<br>2 ft (W) | Modern Shrub Rose<br>Midsummer | ★★★★ | Small<br>5 petals | Pearly pink<br>No fragrance |
| **PENELOPE**<br>The most widely-grown of the healthy, sweet-smelling Hybrid Musk family. Can be kept as a 3 ft bush by annual pruning or grown as a hedge. Dead-head regularly | 1924<br>Spreading | 6 ft (H)<br>x<br>6 ft (W) | Hybrid Musk<br>Repeat flowering | ★★★★ | Small<br>15 petals | Shell pink<br>Fragrant |
| **PERLE D'OR**<br>Similar to Cécile Brunner in general appearance, but the shrub is leafier and more attractive for outdoor bedding. Excellent for cutting | 1884<br>Open | 4 ft (H)<br>x<br>3 ft (W) | China Rose<br>Repeat flowering | ★★ | Small<br>20 petals | Apricot<br>Fragrant |
| **PINK BELLS**<br>One of the modern ground covers — the arching stems clothe the soil surface. White Bells and Red Bells are also available | 1983<br>Procumbent | 2½ ft (H)<br>x<br>4 ft (W) | Modern Shrub Rose<br>Repeat flowering | ★★★ | Small<br>35 petals | Pink<br>Slightly fragrant |
| **PINK GROOTENDORST**<br>A sport of F J Grootendorst — the carnation-like flower feature has been inherited. The colour of the pink form is brighter — a useful hedge for exposed sites | 1923<br>Open | 4½ ft (H)<br>x<br>4½ ft (W) | Rugosa Shrub<br>Repeat flowering | ★★★ | Small<br>25 petals | Rose pink<br>No fragrance |
| **RED BLANKET**<br>A good ground cover — growth is both healthy and vigorous. The foliage is glossy and dark green — highly recommended for hiding old tree stumps etc | 1979<br>Procumbent | 2½ ft (H)<br>x<br>4 ft (W) | Modern Shrub Rose<br>Repeat flowering | ★★★ | Medium<br>10 petals | Rosy red<br>Slightly fragrant |
| **ROSA GALLICA OFFICINALIS**<br>This is the Red Rose of Lancaster — ancestor of many modern reds. The pale red blooms bear prominent yellow stamens. Spray against mildew | pre 1300<br>Upright | 4 ft (H)<br>x<br>3 ft (W) | Gallica Rose<br>Midsummer | ★★ | Medium<br>15 petals | Pale crimson<br>Slightly fragrant |
| **ROSA HUGONIS**<br>A ferny-foliage early-flowering yellow Shrub Rose, like Canary Bird. Not as satisfactory — die-back is a problem and the flowers sometimes fail to open | 1908<br>Arching | 6 ft (H)<br>x<br>6 ft (W) | Species Rose<br>Late spring | ★★★ | Small<br>5 petals | Buttercup yellow<br>Slightly fragrant |
| **ROSA MOYESII GERANIUM**<br>The flowers are rather small for such an imposing bush. It is the hips and not the blooms which are the main attraction — 2 in. long and flagon-shaped | 1938<br>Arching | 8 ft (H)<br>x<br>6 ft (W) | Species Rose<br>Early summer | ★★★ | Small<br>5 petals | Scarlet<br>No fragrance |
| **ROSA MUNDI**<br>A garden rose from 1650 or even 1550, and still a novelty. The blooms, bearing distinct stripes, appear in June or July on a much-branched bush. Spray against mildew | 1650<br>Upright | 4 ft (H)<br>x<br>3 ft (W) | Gallica Rose<br>Midsummer | ★★★★ | Small<br>15 petals | Pale pink, striped crimson<br>No fragrance |
| **ROSA RUBRIFOLIA**<br>A Species Rose widely grown for its purplish foliage and thornless stems rather than for its small and short-lived flowers. The dark red hips are decorative | pre 1830<br>Arching | 6 ft (H)<br>x<br>6 ft (W) | Species Rose<br>Midsummer | ★★★★ | Small<br>5 petals | Pink<br>No fragrance |
| **ROSA RUGOSA ALBA**<br>Flowers are followed by large tomato-like hips in the autumn. A typical Rugosa — wrinkled leaves, tough constitution, fragrant flowers and disease-free leaves | 1870<br>Bushy | 5 ft (H)<br>x<br>5 ft (W) | Rugosa Shrub<br>Repeat flowering | ★★★ | Medium<br>5 petals | White<br>Fragrant |
| **ROSA RUGOSA SCABROSA**<br>Clusters of 5 in. blooms with a carnation-like aroma. These are followed by large red hips in the autumn. An excellent choice for hedging or as a specimen bush | pre 1939<br>Spreading | 5 ft (H)<br>x<br>6 ft (W) | Rugosa Shrub<br>Repeat flowering | ★★ | Large<br>5 petals | Magenta pink<br>Fragrant |

| | | GARDEN RECORD | | | | Included in Rose Analysis |
|---|---|---|---|---|---|---|
| Grown in garden | Year of planting (if known) | Supplier | Performance during the year | Problems during the year | | |
| | | | | | | No |
| | | | | | | OGR |
| | | | | | | OGR |
| | | | | | | No |
| | | | | | | No |
| | | | | | | N |
| | | | | | | No |
| | | | | | | SH |
| | | | | | | No |
| | | | | | | SH |
| | | | | | | No |
| | | | | | | No |
| | | | | | | No |
| | | | | | | No |
| | | | | | | No |
| | | | | | | No |
| | | | | | | No |
| | | | | | | OGR SH |
| | | | | | | SH |
| | | | | | | No |
| | | | | | | SH |

VARIETIES

# SHRUB ROSES

## Varieties

| | PLANT DETAILS | | | | BLOOM DETAILS | |
|---|---|---|---|---|---|---|
| | Year of introduction Growth type | Height (H) x Width (W) | Type Flowering period | Availability | Size of blooms Number of petals | Colour Fragrance |
| **ROSA SERICEA PTERACANTHA** <br> This is the rose with the decorative thorns — red, large and triangular with 1 in.-long bases. The small flowers have little decorative value. Annual pruning is necessary | 1890 <br> Bushy | 8 ft (H) x 6 ft (W) | Species Rose <br> Early summer | ★★★ | Small <br> 4 petals | White <br> No fragrance |
| **ROSERAIE DE L'HAY** <br> A fine bush for the back of the border. Robust, healthy and covered with velvety red flowers in summer and autumn. The only fault is the absence of showy hips | 1902 <br> Bushy | 7 ft (H) x 7 ft (W) | Rugosa Shrub <br> Repeat flowering | ★★★★ | Large <br> 25 petals | Wine red <br> Fragrant |
| **ROSY CUSHION** <br> Similar in general appearance to *Red Blanket*, but the flowers are smaller and much paler. The catalogues recommend the two varieties as partners for edging | 1979 <br> Procumbent | 3 ft (H) x 4 ft (W) | Modern Shrub Rose <br> Repeat flowering | ★★★ | Small <br> 8 petals | Pink; white centre <br> Slightly fragrant |
| **SALLY HOLMES** <br> The trusses are extremely large and often cover the bush. These clusters are borne on long stalks above the foliage. A rather temperamental variety | 1976 <br> Upright | 5 ft (H) x 4 ft (W) | Modern Shrub Rose <br> Repeat flowering | ★★ | Large <br> 5 petals | Creamy white tinged pink <br> Fragrant |
| **SARAH VAN FLEET** <br> This Rugosa Shrub blooms very early and the healthy bush continues to flower all summer. A vigorous plant with dense foliage — excellent for hedging | 1926 <br> Upright | 6 ft (H) x 4 ft (W) | Rugosa Shrub <br> Repeat flowering | ★★★ | Large <br> 20 petals | Pink <br> Very fragrant |
| **SCHNEEZWERG** <br> The flowers are anemone-like. The smallest of the Rugosas listed here, and not the best. Still, the flowering season is long and the hips are attractive | 1912 <br> Spreading | 4 ft (H) x 5 ft (W) | Rugosa Shrub <br> Repeat flowering | ★★★ | Medium <br> 15 petals | White <br> Slightly fragrant |
| **STANWELL PERPETUAL** <br> A good one if you like old-fashioned roses. The blooms, though not large, are filled with petals and perfume. A rambling, untidy bush best grown as a pillar rose | 1838 <br> Arching | 6 ft (H) x 5 ft (W) | Species Rose <br> Repeat flowering | ★★★ | Medium <br> 45 petals | Pale pink <br> Very fragrant |
| **SWANY** <br> A useful ground cover — the fully double blooms are borne in large trusses which stand out against the bronze-tinted glossy leaves | 1978 <br> Procumbent | 1½ ft (H) x 6 ft (W) | Modern Shrub Rose <br> Repeat flowering | ★★★ | Small <br> 50 petals | White <br> Slightly fragrant |
| **THE FAIRY** <br> *The Fairy* remains a popular choice despite the fact that flowering does not start until July. The rosette-shaped blooms are borne in clusters above the box-like foliage | 1932 <br> Spreading | 2½ ft (H) x 2½ ft (W) | Polyantha Rose <br> Repeat flowering | ★★★★ | Small <br> 30 petals | Pale pink <br> No fragrance |
| **UNCLE WALTER** <br> A large bush with velvety H.T-type blooms. Use it as a specimen plant or for hedging — it's too tall for bedding. Disease resistance is good | 1963 <br> Upright | 5 ft (H) x 3 ft (W) | Modern Shrub Rose <br> Repeat flowering | ★★★ | Large <br> 30 petals | Crimson scarlet <br> Slightly fragrant |
| **WILLIAM LOBB** <br> The blooms are beetroot-coloured at first, but soon fade to dull grey. This one needs space to show off the large trusses which open in late June | 1855 <br> Open | 7 ft (H) x 6 ft (W) | Moss Rose <br> Midsummer | ★★★ | Large <br> 30 petals | Purple magenta <br> Fragrant |
| **YESTERDAY** <br> *Yesterday* was an important introduction — it brought back the charm of the old Polyanthas. The flat blooms appear all season long on a compact bush | 1974 <br> Open | 3 ft (H) x 3 ft (W) | Modern Shrub Rose <br> Repeat flowering | ★★★ | Small <br> 15 petals | Pink <br> Fragrant |
| | | | | | | |
| | | | | | | |
| | | | | | | |

**Mary Rose**

**Nevada**

**Red Blanket**

## GARDEN RECORD

| Grown in garden | Year of planting (if known) | Supplier | Performance during the year | Problems during the year | Included in Rose Analysis |
|---|---|---|---|---|---|
| | | | | | No |
| | | | | | SC SH |
| | | | | | No |
| | | | | | SH |
| | | | | | No |
| | | | | | No |
| | | | | | No |
| | | | | | No |
| | | | | | SH |
| | | | | | SH |
| | | | | | No |
| | | | | | No |
| | | | | | |
| | | | | | |
| | | | | | |

VARIETIES

*Rosa Mundi*

*Roseraie de l'Hay*

*The Fairy*

# CHAPTER 3
# CARE

## BUYING ROSES

### BARE ROOT

The traditional type for planting — the bush is dug up at the nursery or garden centre and then sold in one of three ways: over the counter to the waiting customer, put on display with peat around the roots, or packed in a wax-lined bag and posted to the customer. Drying out is a danger — follow the instructions below.

### Bad Signs

Opening leaf buds

Shrivelled stems

Small white roots growing into the peat

### PREPACKAGED

Moist peat is placed around the roots of bare-root plants and the whole plant is then housed in a polythene bag and/or a box. The advantages are reasonable pricing, wide availability and coloured pictures plus instructions. The basic problem is premature growth if the plant has been kept too warm in the shop.

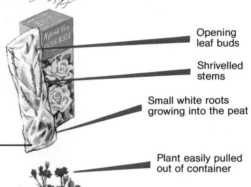

Opening leaf buds

Shrivelled stems

Small white roots growing into the peat

### CONTAINER-GROWN

These plants can be bought all year round, and during the growing season can be used to provide instant colour. Drawbacks include the extra price and the need for extra care at planting time. Look for a sturdy and healthy bush — not one filled with flowers. Make sure it has been grown in the container — not transferred from open ground.

Plant easily pulled out of container

Shrivelled, diseased or bare stems

Thick roots growing out of the container

## GETTING ROSES READY FOR PLANTING

Leave the package containing the bush or standard unopened in an unheated but frost-free cellar, garage or shed. Carefully unpack when you are ready to begin planting. Place the packing material, sacking, etc over the roots. Then prepare each plant as shown in the diagram.

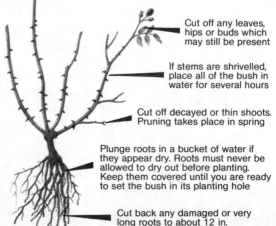

Cut off any leaves, hips or buds which may still be present

If stems are shrivelled, place all of the bush in water for several hours

Cut off decayed or thin shoots. Pruning takes place in spring

Plunge roots in a bucket of water if they appear dry. Roots must never be allowed to dry out before planting. Keep them covered until you are ready to set the bush in its planting hole

Cut back any damaged or very long roots to about 12 in.

### Notes

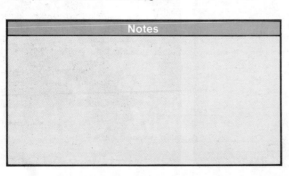

## BUYING OTHER THINGS

Much of the standard gardening equipment in your tool shed or garage will be required when you are working with your roses. The spade, fork, hoe, wheelbarrow, trowel, garden hose and so on all have a role to play. There are a number of items, however, which are used exclusively or mainly in the rose garden, and these are described on this page.

### GLOVES

Gloves are necessary to protect your hands from thorns when pruning and dead-heading. You need both flexibility and stoutness — a good compromise is a pair of fabric gloves with leather palms. Always try on gloves before buying — oversized gloves will result in clumsy handling.

**ESSENTIAL**
✓ when bought

### KNEELING PAD

A kneeling pad will allow you to get close to the bush when the soil is cold and wet at pruning time. Doing any job, such as planting, weeding, pruning etc from a standing position can be a strain on your back. Even better for the elderly is a kneeling frame which can be turned over to serve as a stool.

**ESSENTIAL FOR THE OVER-FIFTIES**
✓ when bought

### SECATEURS

You should need only one pair of secateurs — a general purpose model about 8 in. long. Never economise here — buy the best pair you can afford. Curved secateurs are the most popular type — one sharpened blade cuts against a broad blade. Anvil secateurs have their disciples — one sharpened blade cuts on to a flat platform. Cuts with less effort than the curved type, but the result may be a little ragged and they wear out more quickly.

**ESSENTIAL**
✓ when bought

### PRUNING SAW

Secateurs are not suitable for stems which are more than ½ in. in diameter. Here you will have to use long-handled pruners, but even these are not able to deal with stems which are thicker than a broom handle. The tool for such jobs is a pruning saw. This may have teeth on one or both sides — illustrated here is the Grecian saw.

**DESIRABLE FOR THE SHRUB ROSE ENTHUSIAST**
✓ when bought

### RNRS MEMBERSHIP

For the price of a few rose bushes you can receive all the benefits and privileges enjoyed by a member of The Royal National Rose Society. Application forms are available from The Secretary, The Royal National Rose Society, Chiswell Green, St Albans, Herts AL2 3NR. On joining you will receive copies of HOW TO GROW ROSES and THE ROSE DIRECTORY, and 4 times a year you will receive THE ROSE magazine. In addition there is free admission to the Society's Gardens at St Albans and to many other shows in the U.K.

**ESSENTIAL FOR THE KEEN ROSE GARDENER**
✓ when joined

### FIND THAT ROSE!

Tracking down a supplier of an unusual variety has been a problem for many years. Some roses (e.g *Paris, Black Prince* and *Isobel*) are only grown by one nursery, and finding a rare rose used to be like seeking a needle in a haystack. Now the Rose Growers Association produce a booklet (FIND THAT ROSE!) each year in which the suppliers of more than 2000 varieties are listed. For details write with a stamped addressed envelope to The Editor, 303 Mile End Road, Colchester, Essex CO4 5EA.

**ESSENTIAL FOR THE KEEN ROSE GARDENER**
✓ when bought

### FIRST-AID KIT

Nobody wants a garage filled with a large collection of bottles, boxes and assorted brews. It is, however, a good idea to keep a small rose-aid kit for sudden emergencies. Buy a 1 gallon compression sprayer for general use — never use it for weedkillers. You will need a bottle of systemic insecticide like Long-last for a sudden aphid or caterpillar attack and a box of systemic fungicide (Supercarb) for mildew and black spot. Always read the instructions before using any pesticide, whether natural or chemical.

**ESSENTIAL**
✓ when bought

### THE ROSE EXPERT

For many years THE ROSE EXPERT has been the bible for millions of rose growers, and is now the best-selling rose book in the world. This Jotter covers the same varieties as this book, but there are many additional features. All the rose varieties and all the rose troubles you are ever likely to see are illustrated in colour, and there are sections on rose history, the great rose gardens of the world and rose growing as a hobby.

**ESSENTIAL**
✓ when bought

**CARE**

## PLANTING: CHOOSING THE RIGHT SPOT

✓ if present

- **PLENTY OF SUN** is required to produce top quality roses, but a slight amount of shade during early afternoon is beneficial.

- **SHELTER FROM COLD WINDS IS** helpful. A windbreak such as a nearby hedge or fence is useful, but not if it is close enough to shade the plants.

- **PROTECTION FROM FROST** is necessary for roses described as delicate or non-hardy in the Varieties section. Avoid planting in the lowest part of the garden if it is a 'frost-pocket'.

✓ if present

- **REASONABLY FREE DRAINAGE** is essential, so break up the subsoil if necessary. Roses cannot stand being waterlogged.

- **PLENTY OF FRESH AIR** is required to maintain the health of the plants. Bush and standard roses do not like being shut in by walls and overhanging plants.

- **SUITABLE SOIL IS NECESSARY**, which means the absence of a high lime content or a high raw clay content. Ideally the soil should be a medium loam, slightly acid and reasonably rich in plant foods and humus.

If you have marked 6 ticks, the spot is ideal for roses and you should be able to produce a splendid display provided that you feed, prune and spray as necessary. Three or fewer ticks means that you should think again — roses will not thrive.

## PLANTING: CHOOSING THE RIGHT TIME

|  |  | JAN | FEB | MAR | APR | MAY | JUN | JUL | AUG | SEP | OCT | NOV | DEC |
|---|---|---|---|---|---|---|---|---|---|---|---|---|---|
| **BARE-ROOT PLANTS** November is the best time in nearly all gardens, but March is preferable in very heavy soils and on cold exposed sites. Soil condition is as important as the calendar. The ground must be neither frozen nor waterlogged. Squeeze a handful of soil — it should be wet enough to form a ball and yet hard enough to shatter when dropped on to a hard surface. | **Recommended Planting Time** |  |  |  |  |  |  |  |  |  |  |  |  |
| | **Actual Planting Dates** |  |  |  |  |  |  |  |  |  |  |  |  |
| **CONTAINER-GROWN PLANTS** Any time of the year is suitable, provided the soil is neither frozen nor waterlogged. Spring and autumn are the preferred times. | **Recommended Planting Time** |  |  |  |  |  |  |  |  |  |  |  |  |
| | **Actual Planting Dates** |  |  |  |  |  |  |  |  |  |  |  |  |

## PLANTING: CHOOSING THE RIGHT DISTANCE

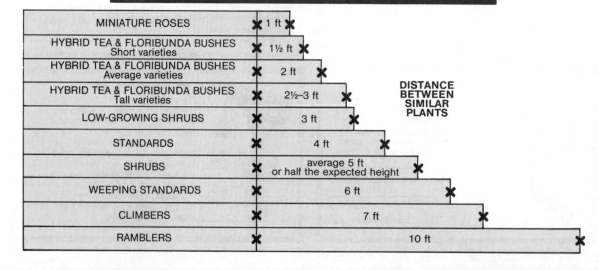

| MINIATURE ROSES | ✖ 1 ft ✖ |
| HYBRID TEA & FLORIBUNDA BUSHES Short varieties | ✖ 1½ ft ✖ |
| HYBRID TEA & FLORIBUNDA BUSHES Average varieties | ✖ 2 ft ✖ |
| HYBRID TEA & FLORIBUNDA BUSHES Tall varieties | ✖ 2½–3 ft ✖ |
| LOW-GROWING SHRUBS | ✖ 3 ft ✖ |
| STANDARDS | ✖ 4 ft ✖ |
| SHRUBS | ✖ average 5 ft or half the expected height ✖ |
| WEEPING STANDARDS | ✖ 6 ft ✖ |
| CLIMBERS | ✖ 7 ft ✖ |
| RAMBLERS | ✖ 10 ft ✖ |

**DISTANCE BETWEEN SIMILAR PLANTS**

# THE PLANTING OPERATION

The first step is to dig the site. Compost, well-rotted manure or peat should be incorporated below the top spit. Remove roots of perennial weeds but do not try to get rid of small stones. Fork 4 oz of Toprose Fertilizer per square yard into the surface soil and let the ground settle for at least 6 weeks before planting. Do not lime soil which is to be used for roses.

This digging operation is not always necessary. If there is a reasonable humus content, good drainage and an absence of perennial weeds, just rake in a little fertilizer and leave it alone. In some situations digging is positively undesirable. For instance, if the topsoil is very shallow and the subsoil is heavy clay, you should add topsoil to produce a raised bed instead of digging.

*Planting Record*

**Notes**

### SPECIAL PREPARATION FOR SITES WHICH HAVE GROWN ROSES FOR MORE THAN 10 YEARS

You may wish to replant an old rose bed or just dig up one or two old bushes and replace them with new ones. In either case the soil is likely to be rose-sick if the plants have been growing in the soil for more than 10 years.

The causes of rose sickness are complex and still not yet fully understood, but a well-known effect is for newly-planted bushes and standards to suffer even though the established roses were thriving before their removal.

It is therefore wise to remove the old soil, digging out a hole 2 ft in diameter and 1½ ft deep for each new plant. Dig in plenty of organic matter and use a planting mixture made up with soil from a part of the garden which has not grown roses in recent years. The old soil from the rose bed can be safely spread in the vegetable or flower garden.

CARE

## Bare-root Plants

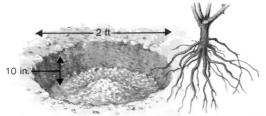

**Round** hole when roots spread out in all directions

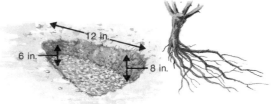

**Fan-shaped** hole when roots run in only one direction

③ Half-fill the hole with more mixture. Tread down lightly. Add more mixture until the hole is full. Tread down lightly, then loosen surface. Add more mixture to cover bud union

① Set plant so that bud union will be 1 in. below surface after planting

**PLANTING MIXTURE**
1 part soil, 1 part moist peat and 3 handfuls of Bone Meal per barrow load

② Place 2 handfuls of planting mixture on top of the mound. Spread out roots evenly and work 2 trowelfuls of planting mixture between them. Shake plant gently up and down — firm soil with your fists

## Container-grown Plants

① Place a layer of planting mixture at the base of the hole

② Water the rose thoroughly before planting. Stand the container in the hole and cut down the side. Gently slide off the cover. Do not lift and do not disturb the soil ball

**PLANTING MIXTURE**
1 part soil, 1 part moist peat and 3 handfuls of Bone Meal per barrow load

③ Fill the space between the soil ball and the sides of the hole with planting mixture. Firm down with the handle of a trowel. Water regularly during dry weather

# PLANTING ARRANGEMENTS

## Beds

A bed is a planted area which is designed to be viewed from all sides. An **island bed** is surrounded by grass or less frequently by gravel or paving — a **flanking bed** divides the lawn from a path or driveway.

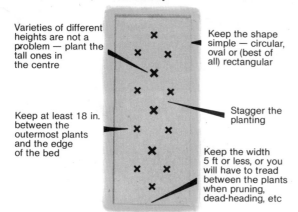

Varieties of different heights are not a problem — plant the tall ones in the centre

Keep the shape simple — circular, oval or (best of all) rectangular

Keep at least 18 in. between the outermost plants and the edge of the bed

Stagger the planting

Keep the width 5 ft or less, or you will have to tread between the plants when pruning, dead-heading, etc

## Borders

A border is a planted area which is designed to be viewed from one, two or three sides but not the back. Shrubs and trees other than roses may be present (**mixed shrub border**) or a selection of perennials may form the background (**mixed herbaceous border**).

Grow Climbers and large Shrubs as single plants

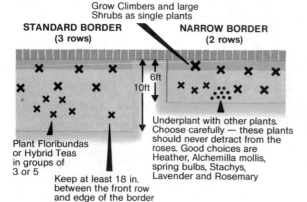

**STANDARD BORDER (3 rows)**

**NARROW BORDER (2 rows)**

6ft
10ft

Plant Floribundas or Hybrid Teas in groups of 3 or 5

Keep at least 18 in. between the front row and edge of the border

Underplant with other plants. Choose carefully — these plants should never detract from the roses. Good choices are Heather, Alchemilla mollis, spring bulbs, Stachys, Lavender and Rosemary

## Hedges

A hedge is a continuous line of bushes in which the individuality of each plant is lost. Unlike a plant-covered fence, a hedge requires little or no support. Roses make an informal hedge — do not try to produce a neat, squared-off outline with shears.

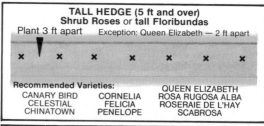

**TALL HEDGE (5 ft and over)**
**Shrub Roses or tall Floribundas**
Plant 3 ft apart      Exception: Queen Elizabeth — 2 ft apart

Recommended Varieties:
CANARY BIRD      CORNELIA      QUEEN ELIZABETH
CELESTIAL      FELICIA      ROSA RUGOSA ALBA
CHINATOWN      PENELOPE      ROSERAIE DE L'HAY
      SCABROSA

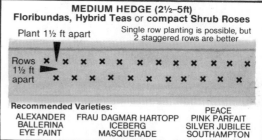

**MEDIUM HEDGE (2½–5ft)**
**Floribundas, Hybrid Teas or compact Shrub Roses**
Plant 1½ ft apart      Single row planting is possible, but 2 staggered rows are better

Rows 1½ ft apart

Recommended Varieties:
      PEACE
ALEXANDER      FRAU DAGMAR HARTOPP      PINK PARFAIT
BALLERINA      ICEBERG      SILVER JUBILEE
EYE PAINT      MASQUERADE      SOUTHAMPTON

**SMALL HEDGE (under 2½ ft)**
**Short Floribundas or Miniature Roses**

## Tubs

A tub is a container (wood, plastic, stone etc) which is large enough and well-drained enough to allow one or more roses to grow successfully. A minimum depth of 9 in. for Miniatures or 12–15 in. for Floribundas and Hybrid Teas is required. As a general rule the most satisfactory tub varieties are the Patio Roses listed on page 2.

## Walls

A wall is a traditional home for Climber or Rambler. Careful choice is essential — pick a variety which is not prone to mildew and make sure you provide proper support. Use vine eyes or rustproof nails and stretch plastic-covered straining wires between them. These lines of wire should be about 1½ ft apart.

## MULCHING

A mulch will greatly reduce the need for watering and hoeing. It is a layer of bulky organic material placed on the soil surface around the plants. The soil is kept moist during summer, weeds are kept down, soil structure is improved and some plant foods may be provided.

Suitable materials are moist peat, well-rotted manure, good garden compost and leaf mould. Do not use weedy lawn clippings nor clippings from a lawn treated with a weedkiller.

Late April or early May is the best time for mulching. Remove debris and weeds, water the surface and spread a 2–3 in. layer around the roses. Keep away from the crowns of the plants.

## WATERING

All roses will need water, and plenty of it, during a period of drought in late spring or summer. Some roses may need watering after only a few days of dry weather — e.g newly-planted roses, Climbers growing against walls and bushes planted in sandy soil.

Never water little and often — use 1 gallon for each bush and 3 gallons for a Climber. Hold the can close to the ground and water slowly through the spout. A quick and easy technique is to build a ridge of soil around each bush and then fill the basin with a hose-pipe.

## HOEING

The main purpose of hoeing is to keep down weeds. It does not reduce water loss by creating a dust mulch. Hoe at regular and frequent intervals — do not go deeper than an inch below the surface.

## DEAD-HEADING

The regular removal of dead blooms from Floribundas and Hybrid Teas is an important task. Remove the whole truss when flowers have faded — cut the stem just above the second or third leaf down. In this way a regular succession of new flowering shoots is ensured. Do not dead-head once-flowering or hip-forming Shrub Roses.

## CUTTING

Roses are widely used as cut flowers for home decoration, but a certain amount of care is necessary to avoid weakening the bushes. Do not take more than one-third of the flowering stem with the flower and always try to cut just above an outward-facing bud. Cutting blooms in the first season after planting is generally not recommended, although the removal of a few blooms without leaves will do no harm.

## DISBUDDING

Many Hybrid Teas produce more than one flower bud at the top of each shoot. Disbudding is necessary if you want a single terminal bloom of maximum size for exhibiting at the show or for arranging. This calls for removing side buds as soon as they appear by nipping out with thumb and finger.

## FEEDING

Roses, like most other garden plants, make heavy demands on the reserves of plant foods in the soil. If one or more of the vital elements runs short, then hunger signs appear. These include small, pale or discoloured leaves, stunted growth, poor quality flowers and low disease resistance.

The answer is to feed your roses every year. A powder or granular fertilizer is the usual form, sprinkled around the plants in spring and summer. Make sure that the fertilizer contains nitrogen, phosphates, potash, magnesium and iron. Liquid fertilizers are a quick-acting alternative — regular repeat treatments are necessary during the season.

A standard feeding programme is to apply a small handful of Toprose around each plant in spring as the leaf buds are opening. Repeat the treatment in June or July. The soil should be moist at the time of treatment — hoe in lightly after feeding. Many exhibitors and keen rose growers enrich this standard programme by spraying the leaves every few weeks with a foliar feed.

## Feeding Record

| Date | Feed | Notes |
|------|------|-------|
|      |      |       |
|      |      |       |
|      |      |       |
|      |      |       |
|      |      |       |
|      |      |       |

CARE

# PRUNING

| | |
|---|---|
| The purpose of pruning is to get rid of old exhausted wood every year and to encourage the development of strong and healthy stems. It will not give you more flowers next year — that is the job of feeding. But it will give you a well-shaped bush which will continue to bloom freely for years to come. | **STEP 1** |
| | **STEP 2** |
| | **STEP 3** |
| | **STEP 4** |

**STEP 1** Cut out completely all dead wood and all parts of stems which are obviously diseased or damaged. Test: Cut surface should be white. If brown — cut back further.

**STEP 2** Cut out completely all very thin stems, and remove any branch which rubs against another. Aim to produce an open-centred bush. Remove suckers.

**STEP 3** Cut out all unripe stems. Test: Try to snap off several thorns. If they bend or tear off instead of breaking off cleanly, the wood is too soft to be of any use.

**STEP 4** Only healthy and ripe stems now remain. Prune these to the length advised on page 57 for the type of rose in question.

## THE PRUNING CUT

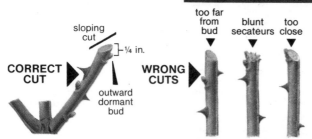

CORRECT CUT — sloping cut — ¼ in. — outward dormant bud

WRONG CUTS — too far from bud — blunt secateurs — too close

All pruning cuts must be clean — pare off any ragged parts. Sharp secateurs are essential — never force them to cut through thick stems, and relegate them to ordinary garden work once the blades are dull. Cuts more than ½ in. across should be painted with Arbrex to protect them from frost and damp.

It is impossible to avoid making some wrong cuts when pruning several bushes on a cold unpleasant day. As a result snags will form above some of the new shoots which develop — merely cut these dead bits off as they appear.

## WHEN TO PRUNE

Prune at or before the recommended pruning date for your part of the country

- EARLY APRIL
- LATE MARCH
- MID MARCH

### BUSHES, STANDARDS & CLIMBERS

Early spring pruning is recommended for autumn- and winter-planted roses and for established plants. If the bushes or standards are to be planted in the spring, prune just before planting.

The best time to prune is when growth is just beginning. The uppermost buds will have begun to swell but no leaves will have appeared.

One of the dangers of leaving pruning until spring is the possibility of wind-rock in the winter gales. Avoid this by cutting back long shoots in November.

### RAMBLERS

Prune in late summer or autumn once flowering has finished.

**Pruning too early** may result in buds breaking prematurely in a mild spell, followed by frost injury if freezing weather returns.

Despite this possibility, some rose experts prune regularly during above-freezing weather in January or February and claim they obtain earlier flowering than with the more usual March pruning.

**Pruning too late** results in the plant being weakened. This is because the sap is flowing freely upwards once the buds are actively growing, and pruning at this stage is bound to cause considerable loss of sap.

## Pruning Record

| Date | Notes |
|---|---|
| | |
| | |
| | |
| | |
| | |
| | |
| | |

## TYPES OF PRUNING

# Hybrid Teas & Floribundas

| BEFORE | AFTER | TYPE |
|---|---|---|
| | | **HARD PRUNING**<br>*(other name: Low Pruning)*<br>Stems are cut back to three or four buds from the base. This leaves short, sturdy stems about 5 in. high.<br>Hard pruning is recommended for newly-planted bush roses and it is often used for established H.Ts grown solely for the production of exhibition blooms.<br>It is no longer recommended for established roses grown for garden display although it is still used for some very weak-growing H.Ts and for rejuvenating neglected roses. Hard pruning should never be used for established Floribundas. |
| | | **MODERATE PRUNING**<br>*(other name: Medium Pruning)*<br>Stems are cut back to about half of their length. Weaker than average stems should be reduced by more than this amount. Moderate pruning is recommended for nearly all established H.Ts growing in ordinary soils.<br>Established Floribundas are pruned using a variation of this system. Most stems are moderately pruned — some old stems are hard pruned to a few inches from the ground, whilst new shoots which arose from close to the base last year are lightly pruned. In this way stems of various lengths are retained and this ensures a long flowering period. |
| | | **LIGHT PRUNING**<br>*(other name: High or Long Pruning)*<br>Stems are cut back to about two-thirds of their length. This means that after the removal of all unwanted wood, the remaining stems are merely tipped.<br>Light pruning is not generally recommended as it produces tall spindly bushes bearing early but poor quality blooms if used year after year.<br>In special cases, however, light pruning is the only method to use. Very vigorous H.T varieties such as *Peace* should be tackled in this way, and all roses growing in very sandy or smoky areas should be lightly pruned. |

# Shrubs & Miniatures

Very little pruning is required. Remove dead and sickly growth and then trim to shape if necessary. Remove and burn mildewed tips. Use scissors rather than secateurs for Miniatures.

# Climbers

Little pruning is required apart from the removal of dead and exhausted wood. Withered shoot tips should be removed. With a few varieties (*Casino, Climbing Ena Harkness, Mermaid, Parkdirektor Riggers* and *Climbing Shot Silk*) lateral branches on wood which has flowered should be reduced to about 3 in.

# Ramblers

Ideally, all the stems which have flowered should be cut in autumn to either ground level or to the union with the main stem, depending on the variety. In practice, taking down so much wood is not usually practical. In this case just cut back the lateral branches to about 3 in. from the main stems. With a few varieties (*Emily Gray, Félicité et Perpétue* and *Rosa Filipes Kiftsgate*) only very light pruning is required — merely cut out dead wood and tip back laterals which have flowered.

CARE

## CULTURAL PROBLEMS

### IRON SHORTAGE
Large yellow areas — young leaves worst affected. Apply Toprose — use MultiTonic on chalky soils

### MAGNESIUM SHORTAGE
Pale at centre with dead areas close to midrib — old leaves worst affected. Apply a rose fertilizer containing magnesium

### FROST DAMAGE
Crinkled and torn with brown markings. Not usually serious, but in N. areas winter protection may be needed

### BALLING
Buds develop normally, but petals fail to open and turn brown. Caused by prolonged rain on large, thin-petalled flowers

### WEEDKILLER DAMAGE
Leaf stalks twisted, leaves narrow and twisted. Caused by lawn weedkiller drift. Remove affected stems

## PESTS

### GREENFLY
Greenfly (Aphid) is the most serious of all rose pests. The first clusters feed on new shoots in the spring. Growth is distorted — infested buds may fail to open. Spray with a systemic, e.g Long-last

### CUCKOO-SPIT
Frothy spittle in May or June — inside this froth lives the small yellow Froghopper. Leaves may wilt. If only a few shoots are affected, wipe off with finger or thumb. Hexyl is effective — spray with water first

### ROSE SCALE
Small scurfy scales form a crust on old and neglected stems. Unsightly, and growth is weakened. Wipe off small areas with methylated spirits. Spray large areas with Long-last

### BLINDNESS
An empty wheat-like husk instead of a flower bud on top of a mature stem. Any check to growth (frost, starvation etc) can cause it. Some varieties such as *Peace* are particularly prone

### COCKCHAFER
Irregular-shaped holes in leaves during May and June may be due to this large, reddish-brown beetle — the Maybug. Pick off and destroy the beetles. Spray, if necessary, with Long-last

### CATERPILLAR
A number of caterpillars (e.g Vapourer moth, Winter moth and Buff-tip moth) produce irregular-shaped holes in leaves. Pick off by hand if not too numerous. Spray, if necessary, with Long-last

### ROSE SLUGWORM
Easily recognised — skeletonised areas appear on the leaves, as only the soft tissues and not the veins are eaten. Greenish-yellow grub may be seen on the surface. Spray with Long-last or Derris

### LEAFHOPPER
Pale mottled patches on leaves. Small yellowish insects or their white skins may be found on the underside. Leaf fall may occur after a bad attack. Spray with Long-last or Sprayday

### RED SPIDER
Bronzed patches on upper surface — minute yellowish mites and fine webbing on the underside. Attacks occur in hot, dry weather. Spraying may be necessary in midsummer — use Long-last or Malathion

### CHAFER BEETLE
The Rose chafer and Garden chafer eat the petals and anthers — one-sided blooms are produced. Pick off and destroy the beetles. They can be controlled by spraying with Long-last

### TORTRIX MOTH
Holes appear in the leaves, but the tell-tale sign is the fine silken thread which ties the edges of the leaflets together. Pick and destroy affected leaves. Long-last will prevent damage

### LEAF-ROLLING SAWFLY
Leaflets are tightly rolled with a greyish-green grub inside. Affected leaves may shrivel and die. Squeeze rolled leaflets between thumb and finger. Spray with Long-last to prevent damage

# DISEASES

### MILDEW

Mildew is the most widespread of all rose diseases. It attacks in summer or early autumn, covering leaves and buds with white, powdery mould. It is not fatal, but leaves cockle and may fall prematurely. It is encouraged by soil dryness, poor fertility, hot days followed by cold nights and by enclosed conditions. Spray with Multirose or Supercarb — repeat 1 week later and then apply further sprays if mould reappears

### BLACK SPOT

A serious disease — severe leaf loss can take place and shoots may die back. The black spots on the leaves are easily recognised in July or August, but the disease starts in spring. It is encouraged by clean air, potash shortage and warm, wet weather. Difficult to control. Spray with Multirose or Supercarb when leaf buds begin to open — repeat 1 week later and then again in summer when spots appear

### RUST

Not a common problem, but it is often fatal when it occurs. Orange swellings appear in July on the underside of the foliage — these pustules turn black in August. New shoots turn reddish and shrivel. It is encouraged by potash deficiency and by a cold spring followed by a dry summer and frosty winter. Prevention is the best plan if you live in a rust-prone area — spray with Dithane every 2 weeks

### DIE-BACK

Shoots die back, beginning at the tip and progressing steadily downwards. Yellow and orange varieties seem to be more susceptible than others. There is no single cause — it is linked with frost or disease damage and also with poor drainage. It is encouraged by nutrient deficiency — always feed in spring if die-back is a problem. Remove each affected shoot by cutting at a bud below the affected area

# SPRAYING

● BEFORE SPRAYING Choose the product carefully. Make sure that the problem is mentioned on the label. Insecticides should be used at the first sign of attack. A systemic insecticide enters the sap stream and so can reach insects which are hidden from the spray. Fungicides prevent rather than cure diseases, so early spraying is vital. Systemic fungicides enter the sap stream. Always read the label carefully and follow the instructions and precautions.

● SPRAYING Choose a day which is neither sunny nor windy, and choose a time in summer which is late in the day so that bees will not be harmed. Make up the spray as directed — never use equipment which has contained weedkillers. Use a fine forceful spray to cover the top and underside of the foliage — continue until the liquid starts to run off the leaves. Try to keep all sprays off the skin. If splashes occur, wash the affected area immediately.

● AFTER SPRAYING Wash out equipment thoroughly. Do this straight away — do not leave the chemical to dry inside the nozzle. Wash your hands and face if the label tells you to do so. Do not pour left-over spray into a bottle for use next time — you should make up a fresh batch of solution each time you wish to treat your roses. Store containers in a safe place away from pets and children. Never transfer chemicals into bottles — throw old containers into the dustbin after disposing of the contents safely.

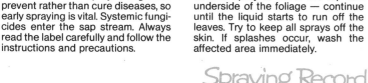

Spraying Record

| Date | Problem | Pesticide used | Comments |
|------|---------|----------------|----------|
|      |         |                |          |
|      |         |                |          |
|      |         |                |          |
|      |         |                |          |
|      |         |                |          |

**CHAPTER 4**

# DIARY

## JANUARY

There is usually little to do in the rose garden this month — midwinter frosts can make January a bad time for planting in many areas. Inspect autumn-planted roses — frost may have loosened them. Firm if necessary. Check the ties on roses growing on supports. Beds to be planted in March should be prepared this month.

## FEBRUARY

Like January, this month is generally a bad time for planting. However, this work can continue in light soil if the temperature is above freezing. In mild districts the pruning of vigorous Floribundas can begin at the end of the month. Stocks budded last year can be cut back.

## MARCH

For many rose growers March heralds in the start of the year. This is the best time to plant bare-root roses in heavy soil areas and some consider March the best time for pruning bush and standard roses. Burn all prunings.

Feeding can begin this month, but it is usually better to wait until April. Weed beds thoroughly — apply a simazine-based weedkiller if hoeing is not practical. Apply a weekly liquid feed to pot roses in the greenhouse.

## APRIL

Roses will start to grow actively. Pruning must be completed by the beginning of the month — rub out any surplus young shoots. Apply a fertilizer, such as Toprose, around the bushes. Keep the powder off new growth and lightly prick into the soil surface.

In areas which are prone to black spot the first fungicide application should be made as soon as the leaf buds start to open. Apply two carbendazim sprays a week apart. Neaten bed edges.

## MAY

Roses will now be growing rapidly. The first of the early-flowering Shrub Roses will start to flower. This is the month to put down a mulch around the stems — make sure the surface is moist and weed-free before spreading the organic material.

Greenfly attacks are likely, and a systemic insecticide which works through the sap stream is the best method of control. Apply a foliar feed such as Fillip to backward plants. Visit the Chelsea Flower Show in London.

## JUNE

The bushes and standards will now be coming into flower. Hoe, spray and water as necessary. Cut flowers for indoor decoration from established plants — not from newly-planted bushes.

Disbud Hybrid Teas (see page 55) if you want top-quality blooms of maximum size. This is the time to apply a summer feed. It is also the time to obtain a schedule if you plan to enter your roses at the local show. Apply a mixed insecticide/fungicide spray.

## JULY

The bushes and standards should now be in full flower — this is the peak month for display. Dead-head as necessary, and apply a summer feed if this was not done last month.

Hoe, disbud, mulch and water as noted for June. Keep a special watch for mildew — spray as soon as the first white spots are seen. If you are going away on holiday, remove all flowers which have begun to fade so that hips will not form during your absence. Bud rootstocks this month. Visit the British Rose Festival at St Albans.

## AUGUST

Hoeing, spraying, watering, disbudding and dead-heading continue this month as they did in July but there is one difference — feeding should not continue in August.

Start to think about next year. Visit nurseries to see the newer varieties in bloom — this is better than relying on catalogue descriptions. Go to see Display Gardens if you can — there are a number of them around the country. Send off your order for new introductions as soon as possible, as they do tend to sell out early.

DIARY

## SEPTEMBER

Most bushes will still be flowering freely, and dead-heading is essential to prolong the display. Continue hoeing and spraying as necessary — Ramblers and weeping standards should have been pruned by now.

This is the time to prepare new beds for November planting. Send off your rose order. This is a good month for taking cuttings of Ramblers and vigorous Floribundas. Visit the Rose Festival in London — many local autumn rose shows are staged this month.

## OCTOBER

Now is the time to tidy up the beds. Collect up and burn fallen leaves and hoe in the mulching material. Finish preparing the new beds and borders. Nurseries start to send out their plants in October and planting can start at the end of the month. Read the section on planting (see pages 52–54) if you are inexperienced.

Pot roses grown under glass are repotted this month. Pots which have been stood outdoors are brought inside at the end of October.

## NOVEMBER

The show is over for another year and the plants must be got ready for the winter. Long stems should be cut back a little in exposed areas to prevent windrock during winter storms. In really cold districts it is wise to earth-up the plants with straw.

November is an excellent time for planting. If the bushes or standards arrive during a spell of bad weather, leave the packages unopened until you are ready. Plant in a temporary spot ('heel-in') if the delay is likely to be prolonged.

## DECEMBER

In most years the soil gets progressively wetter and colder, so try to complete your planting as early in the month as possible. Never try to plant when the soil is waterlogged or frost-bound.

The work in established rose beds and borders should have been completed in November, but work can begin on the preparation of new beds for March planting. Pot roses in the greenhouse should be pruned and kept fairly dry — keep the temperature above freezing if heat is available.

# CHAPTER 5

# INDEX

### Acknowledgements

The author wishes to acknowledge the painstaking work of Gill Jackson, Jane Llewelyn and John Woodbridge. Grateful acknowledgement is also made to Angela Pawsey, Lt.Col Ken Grapes, Constance Barry, Carolyn Lathrope, Joan Hessayon, Linda Fensom, Angelina Gibbs, Rosemary McCarthy, Susan McCarthy, Dick Balfour, Cants of Colchester, James Cocker & Sons, Dickson Nurseries Ltd., Fryer's Nurseries Ltd., C. Gregory & Son Ltd., John Mattock Ltd., Rosemary Roses, Sealand Nurseries Ltd., Harry Smith Horticultural Photographic Collection, Wheatcroft Roses Ltd. and the Royal National Rose Society. Mike Standage prepared the paintings for this book.